# MISSING PIECES

# MISSING PIECES

7 Ways to Improve Employee
Well-Being and Organizational
Effectiveness

**Jean-Pierre Brun**

*Professor of Management, Université Laval in Canada*

**Cary Cooper**

*Pro Vice Chancellor (External Relations) and Professor of*
*Organizational Psychology and Health,*
*Lancaster University*

First published 2009 by
PALGRAVE MACMILLAN

Palgrave Macmillan in the UK is an imprint of Macmillan Publishers Limited,
registered in England, company number 785998, of Houndmills, Basingstoke,
Hampshire RG21 6XS.

Palgrave Macmillan in the US is a division of St Martin's Press LLC,
175 Fifth Avenue, New York, NY 10010.

Palgrave Macmillan is the global academic imprint of the above companies
and has companies and representatives throughout the world.

Palgrave® and Macmillan® are registered trademarks in the United States,
the United Kingdom, Europe and other countries

ISBN-13: 978–0–230–57658–2
ISBN-10: 0–230–57658–3

This book is printed on paper suitable for recycling and made from fully
managed and sustained forest sources. Logging, pulping and manufacturing
processes are expected to conform to the environmental regulations of the
country of origin.

A catalogue record for this book is available from the British Library.

A catalog record for this book is available from the Library of Congress.

10  9  8  7  6  5  4  3  2  1
18  17  16  15  14  13  12  11  10  09

Printed and bound in China

*For Evelyn and Étienne*
*For Rachel, Scott, Beth, Laura and Sarah*

# CONTENTS

CONTENTS

# ACKNOWLEDGMENTS

Our thanks go to the managers and employees of businesses we have worked hand in hand with over the years. This book is about their efforts to improve employee well-being and business efficiency. We wish to thank them for their trust and the challenges we had to rise to.

# INTRODUCTION

This book answers the question: *What is missing from management when employees are unhappy and organizations inefficient?*

In the course of our[1] careers, we have been lucky to work with some remarkable senior executives, managers, union representatives and ordinary employees who think employee well-being and business efficiency go hand in hand. They have asked us for help while explaining their responsibilities, describing the pros and cons of their duties and outlining the solutions they have tried.

We have also surveyed thousands of people, interviewed hundreds of managers, met with hundreds of workers in trouble-shooting sessions, and counseled dozens of management committees, boards of directors and union groups. We have been involved in the aeronautic, transportation and metallurgy industries and active with leading financial institutions, pharmaceutical consumer groups, retailers, government departments, hospitals and food chains. We have observed many working people go about their jobs: call center attendants, senior managers, nurses, construction workers, reporters, linemen, human resources advisers, accountants, social workers and teachers. We have given hundreds of talks and provided dozens of corporate training programs. Our numerous encounters with employees and managers have convinced us that many problems are due to what we call *missing pieces* in the way we manage employees and organizations. Here are a few examples:

- A dental assistant complains that her boss is out of the office and shows next to no recognition for staff performance
- A team leader says she is overwhelmed by the number of files she must handle and adds she has no way of getting her supervisor to assess or even discuss the workload
- A 55-year-old human resources adviser says he has little leeway in tackling complex labor issues and is seldom allowed to make decisions on his own
- A production manager complains how hard it is to allocate budgets among different departments because her company's priorities are too vague
- An occupational health-and-safety manager is fed up with the lack of team spirit among her staff. She places the blame squarely on management for lack of support, assistance and cooperation
- A nurse is unhappy with doing overtime, which interferes with her family life
- A foreman claims he is being harassed at work and says his director is offering no recourse or support.

Our experiences have shown that many workers and managers like their jobs, but a growing number find their working conditions intolerable. What are the obstacles to a rewarding work environment and an efficient business? What are the alternatives? How can organizations solve these problems while ensuring their long-term survival?

When writing this book, we wanted to share our experiences and knowledge about barriers to making employees happier and organizations more efficient. Its focus is on day-to-day work, which is so poorly acknowledged in the business world. While the daily grind may seem less "trendy" or "strategic" than leadership and corporate strategies, it matters as much to success.

We increasingly believe that a healthy and efficient company differs from a sick and inefficient one, not only in standard business strategies to attract, retain and properly pay employees but also in working conditions. The same point has been made by many well-known writers. Warren Bennis, for one, says that leadership accounts for no more than 15 percent of an organization's success, with 85 percent depending on the efforts of the tens, hundreds and even thousands of people who daily do its work.

Other writers, such as Richard Templar, James O'Toole, Aubreys C. Daniels and Arie De Geus, similarly see a close tie between employee well-being and business efficiency. These two factors are closely related in the daily work of employees and managers. So, when people complain about their well-being on the job, it comes as no surprise that 95 percent of the time they really mean problems with business efficiency.

Take the case of a hospital radiology department. Several employees told us they had not had a staff meeting in five years. They felt irrelevant, outside the loop and lacking in managerial support.

While speaking with them, we learned they had not received any recognition for their work. They had become demoralized, isolated and increasingly stressed out.

This situation affected not only their sense of well-being but also their performance. Mistakes often happened; X-ray reports disappeared; staff members were uncooperative with each other; no one was willing to make the slightest effort to help their boss; and patients were complaining about lack of staff courtesy.

Meanwhile, the manager said she had too much work and too little time or energy. She knew the team was below par and had a lot of trouble doing the job right. She also had no idea how to turn things around.

As this brief example shows, such situations may impair employee well-being and business efficiency. That is why it pays to improve the working conditions of employees and managers. In any event, this is a necessity for organizations and administrators. A company is entitled to ask its employees to do their best, but it must also provide the conditions for good job performance.

## ABOUT THIS BOOK

This book describes the pieces missing in management of human capital and organizations and sets out a simple and tangible way to find the effective and long-lasting solutions.

The first chapter outlines what we mean by "missing pieces of management." It also explains the concept of organizational health. Chapter 2 addresses the key issue of recognition in the workplace. Chapter 3 stresses the importance of social support and interpersonal relations. Chapter 4 covers the delicate issue of respect in the workplace. Chapter 5 discusses reconciliation between work and personal life, a popular topic these days. Chapter 6 is about workload. Chapter 7 deals with employee autonomy and participation in decision making. Chapter 8 goes into ambiguity and conflict in employee roles. Chapter 9 is on matching words with acts and concludes by defining a simple yet effective way to make changes that will fill in the missing pieces of management.

We hope this book will not only lead to further thought and dialogue but also help people move from words to acts. As a manager, you will find much information on changing your organization's working conditions, management practices and leadership strategies.

Because this book deals with sensitive issues, we have concealed identities and altered details to ensure confidentiality. The quotes, however, are verbatim, and the situations are accurately portrayed.

Each chapter concludes with two sections to help you enhance employee well-being and business efficiency. The first one, "What's your situation?" shows you how to assess your own organization, and see how it ranks in terms of missing pieces. The second section, "10 simple actions," provides simple solutions you can apply.

You may read this book from start to finish, or begin with the sections that interest you most. It is designed as a guide to help you think through these issues and as a management resource for better workplaces and more efficient businesses.

We hope our book will bring these missing pieces to mind whenever you draw up plans, develop marketing practices and set standards for working conditions.

# CHAPTER 1

# DISCOVER THE MISSING PIECES OF MANAGEMENT

Most large organizations are very sick.

—Peter Senge

## WHAT ARE THE MISSING PIECES?

Take a few moments to think over this question. What do people really mean by "employee well-being"? Beyond the problems that apply to each job, work unit or organization, you will often hear such comments in the workplace as: "If we had . . . ," "We're missing . . . ," "We often forget the individual . . . ," "I'm not . . . " and so forth.

Ask people what is missing in their jobs. Most will talk about different things that amount to inadequate working conditions. They will mention the deficiencies in management, the "little extra" that is required, the human dimension that is lacking or the labor and management practices that have disappeared over the years. In listening to such comments, we have come to the realization that problems in improving well-being on the job are due to factors that are absent from management—what we call "missing pieces."

The problems, or missing pieces, that emerge most often from our analysis are listed below and are discussed in separate chapters.

| The 7 missing pieces | Definition |
|---|---|
| 1. Recognition at work | Expressing appreciation to employees genuinely and constructively. Such recognition is given primarily for the way they carry out their responsibilities, for their efforts and energy, for the results they achieve, for their contributions and for their human qualities. |
| 2. Social support | Being able to go to trustworthy individuals for assistance and advice in times of emotional difficulty. |
| 3. Respect at work | Behaving in a way that preserves mutually acceptable standards of courtesy on the job and includes positive and constructive interactions with others. Respect promotes cooperation and the development of long-term relationships. |
| 4. Work/life balance | Creating a situation where improvements in one area of your life (personal or professional) will spill over into the other. |
| 5. Workload | The job to be done (in terms of quantity, pace, intensity and deadline) and its accompanying effects (fatigue, effort, trouble concentrating and wear and tear). Cumulative effort (task + effect) will affect the individual (stress, demoralization and isolation) and business efficiency. |
| 6. Participation in decision making | Having leeway and flexibility in deciding how the work should be done, being able to influence the level of responsibility, having opportunities to participate in decision making and giving feedback on information from an immediate supervisor. Participation in decision |

*Continued*

8

*Continued*

| The 7 missing pieces | Definition |
| --- | --- |
| | making also includes being able to apply creative solutions and develop personal abilities. |
| 7. Role conflict or role ambiguity | "Role conflict" is a state of mind or perception caused by conflicting demands, where fulfillment of one will impede or block another. "Role ambiguity" in the workplace is a perception that your role, schedules and work methods have been poorly defined. |

As mentioned, each missing piece of management will be discussed in a separate chapter, but relationships do exist between them. Overwork, for instance, may trigger problems with other employees, or adversely affect home life. Lack of involvement in decision making might reduce one's sense of personal recognition. Role ambiguity could weaken employee autonomy. Such examples will show the importance of a systems approach to problem solving throughout this book.

One reason why pieces are missing is that employee well-being is seldom felt to be important. It is only an occasional item on the agendas of senior executives and managers.

This disinterest is evident in a 2002 study of 269 finance directors by the Integrated Benefits Institute. Almost all respondents (9 out of 10) saw a direct link between employee well-being and productivity. The study's authors then asked the respondents to list their usual management indicators. It turned out that the three key ones were cash flow, sales and benefits. There was no mention of any indicators for employee well-being!

## WHAT IS A HEALTHY BUSINESS?

> The health of employees cannot be considered separately from that of the company.
>
> (Johnson & Johnson)

A "healthy business" should place employee well-being on the same level as other goals, and include it in its management criteria. This means more than just putting employee well-being on a list of values or priorities. Businesses tend to focus on a few things (quality, productivity, technological change), while letting others go unnoticed. They need to avoid this pitfall by making employee well-being a managerial key performance indicator (KPI) and a criterion of decision making. It is important to put it on a par with liquidity, sales and benefits.

A healthy business will need much more than programs that offer such activities as yoga, chair massage, stress management and nutritional information. While such activities are not necessarily harmful, they will have no long-term impact and will not eliminate risks to employee well-being.

A healthy business is a place where you can build up your health, and not wear it down. The health impact will depend on the mix of conditions in the work environment. Some mixes may be toxic, such as overwork coupled with lack of recognition or lack of opportunity to participate in decision making. Others, such as good social support along with adequate autonomy and clear definition of responsibilities, are conducive to health.

How do we define a "healthy business"? What criteria should we use?

First, a healthy business has rules, guidelines, procedures, resources and practices that promote the employee's physical and mental health. In turn, healthy employees will help the business meet its goals for production or service, for efficiency and for corporate well-being.

A business is not necessarily "healthy" if its workforce has fewer accidents and illnesses, or a low rate of absenteeism. Such a distinction is crucial. We often meet managers and human resource or occupational health-and-safety experts who believe that no news is good news (i.e., no accidents, illnesses or absences). Then there are those who feel they have a "healthy business," once it has introduced a problem-management system.

Let us repeat: an organization is not healthy simply because there are no risk factors such as overwork, conflict, lack of autonomy, or work-related accidents or illnesses. Its health is defined by the "presence and quality of management practices," and "working conditions that promote well-being."

Several internationally renowned experts[1] have spelled out the **four defining principles** of a "healthy business":

*Principle 1: Health is a continuum that runs from well-being to death.* Businesses must not only seek to prevent illness or death, but also deal with the adverse consequences of such situations, while also promoting health.

*Principle 2: A sound business is a process, not a stable condition.* Keeping it sound is an ongoing effort. Employee health, in particular, should be treated as a managerial duty, like accounting, marketing or quality control. When perceived in this way, employee health will become an ongoing organizational function.

*Principle 3: Health should be viewed as part of a comprehensive systems approach.* Being healthy on the job will depend, in short, on interconnections and relationships with different organizational, social, economic and individual factors. The existing system should take this holistic approach into account and shield itself from risks.

*Principle 4: Healthy businesses have a culture of cooperation and constant communication.* Such principles will enable the employees and the employer to engage in constructive dialogue on building and maintaining the foundations of a healthy business.

Finally, several studies have shown a positive correlation between employee well-being and business efficiency. Here are the key findings:

- Level of employee satisfaction is reflected in punctuality and rates of absenteeism.[2]
- Employee satisfaction is related to employee commitment.[3]
- Employee commitment is associated with low turnover and high performance.[4]
- Half of all absences from work are associated with an unhealthy or stressful work environment.[5]
- Customer satisfaction directly correlates with employee satisfaction.[6]

- Satisfaction with job security and pay, and satisfaction in general, correlate with a company's financial performance.[7]

The interrelationships between employee well-being, employee performance and productivity have been well documented over the past decade. Specialists now recognize a very strong causal link between employee well-being and business efficiency. This relationship will turn positive if the missing pieces described throughout this book are put back into your management practices.

## WHAT'S YOUR SITUATION?

There are certain rules for success in improving employee well-being and business efficiency. The key ones are listed below. Read through the diagnostic chart to get a feel for your situation, and how you can promote well-being and efficiency.

## DIAGNOSTIC CHART

| | | |
|---|---|---|
| 100% | = | We often take the lead in this practice—There is room for improvement, but very little. |
| 80% | = | We take the lead in this practice—There is some room for improvement. |
| 70% | = | We offer little leadership in this practice—We should improve. |
| 50% | = | We are not leaders in this practice—There is clearly room for improvement. |
| 30% | = | We are not at all leaders in this practice—There is a lot of room for improvement. |

| | Leader, manager and worker practices | Score (%) |
|---|---|---|
| **Leader Practices** | 1. Senior executives recognize the relationship between employee well-being and business efficiency. | — |
| | 2. Senior executives use a system to manage risks, to organize prevention strategies and to control the costs of employee well-being. | — |
| **Manager Practices** | 3. Managers integrate concerns about employee well-being into their daily management. | — |
| | 4. Managers are also assessed on their performance in ensuring employee well-being. | — |
| **Worker Practices** | 5. Employees care about their own well-being and that of coworkers. | — |
| | 6. Employees actively promote a healthy, risk-free work environment. | — |

Once you have completed your company diagnosis, talk it over with relevant people in your organization (board of directors, management committee, work group, team meeting, etc.), to enhance awareness of your situation and then to draw up an action plan on employee well-being and business efficiency. These discussions will generate ideas and feedback that will certainly assist you in planning and initiating changes.

# 10 Simple Actions

## 1. Measure absenteeism

Although absenteeism is generally measured as the number of workdays lost, such figures underestimate

14

the actual cost and impact. Other indicators will help give you a broader idea of how absenteeism affects your company:

- people receiving disability payments
- excessive overtime
- lengthy delay in returning to work
- medical assessments by company doctor or nurse
- high employee turnover.

## 2. Measure presenteeism
"Presenteeism" is the reduced performance of an employee who continues to work even with health problems. It may be measured by

- increase in the number of mistakes
- reduction in the quality of production
- employee assistance program (EAP) enrolment
- medical assessments by noncompany personnel
- legal claims
- loss of productivity.

## 3. Make employee health a management criterion
Health may be a priority or a value but is above all a criterion of management decision making. It is a managerial duty that concerns all company departments and not just human resources or the medical service. It should be one of the keys to business decision making and success.

## 4. Factor in both direct and indirect costs
Direct costs (employment insurance and absenteeism) are only the tip of the iceberg when it comes to the actual cost of an unhealthy work environment. There are also indirect costs that need to be estimated to

portray the situation fairly and realistically. Indirect costs include presenteeism, loss of expertise, cost of replacing workers and longer lead times.

5. **Treat work as a health factor**
   Work takes up a big chunk of our daily lives—more than half our waking time, in fact. We also know that work is good for our psychological health, because the workplace is conducive to social interaction, recognition and self-actualization. Working conditions are not, however, always geared to health and well-being. By eliminating certain barriers (lack of recognition, overwork, etc.), you will help promote the personal development of your employees, while preventing harm to their sense of well-being.

6. **Broaden your vision of employee health**
   Employee health has usually meant accidents and illnesses at work. This is a negative definition and implies that a workplace is healthy if there are no accidents or illnesses. This is untrue. Latent risks may persist or delayed effects may be felt long after an accident. Health is not only an absence of illness but also a presence of well-being and balance with the work environment.

7. **Do not focus just on cutting costs**
   The primary reason for putting back "the missing pieces of management" is to improve the well-being and efficiency of your company. Controlling costs is secondary. Of course, there must be concern about costs but it should not be the only factor in motivating managers and employees to take an active part in improving working conditions. The risk in focusing on costs is that you may become less vigilant once costs

are under control. Usually this is when real problems begin.

8. **Remember that working conditions may be changed**
   "Work" and "business" have always been evolving concepts. Over time, technologies have advanced, production processes have been upgraded and human resource management has become increasingly effective. Work can likewise be changed to make it more conducive to employee health.

9. **Make a healthy business an organizational goal**
   Employee well-being is a criterion of business efficiency and performance. Maintaining a healthy company should not simply be a goal of occupational health or the human resources department. It should also be a business goal supported by senior executives, including the CEO, the directors and so forth. Being a healthy company is a goal to be shared at all levels of management.

10. **Face the facts**
    Economic performance goes with a healthy work environment. To know how healthy this environment is, you will need clear analysis, which must begin by candidly going over each item. The facts must be laid out and the company, not the employees, must shoulder responsibility for any problems. Blaming the employees will only maintain the status quo and make it harder to improve working conditions and, hence, business performance. By confronting reality, and not simply diagnosing it, analysis lays the groundwork for future actions.

## KEY POINTS

- When asked to explain what is wrong with their jobs, most people will talk about what is missing from their working conditions
- Indicators of employee health rarely appear in the reports of business managers or executives
- Managers will become more concerned about employee well-being if it is made a managerial KPI and a criterion of management or business decision making
- A healthy company has guidelines, rules, procedures and practices that serve to promote the physical and mental well-being of its employees. Such improvements will in turn contribute to its own efficiency and the well-being of society
- A healthy company seeks not only to prevent accidents and illnesses but also to promote a healthy workplace and healthy employees
- A company's health is measured not solely by the absence of risk factors or illness, but also by the quality of its management practices and by working conditions that promote health
- An ever-increasing number of studies reveal that company health is reflected in healthier employees, less absenteeism, higher productivity, better service quality and increased competitiveness

# CHAPTER 2

# RECOGNIZE YOUR EMPLOYEES: A SIMPLE ACT

Gratitude is the heart's memory.

—Hans Christian Andersen

After visiting a call center to introduce practices for better recognition of its 250 employees, we were told by one: "This is the first time in 15 years on the job that a vice-president has come and sat down with me for an hour to get a better understanding of what I do! He was nice and showed interest in my work. He saw it wasn't easy to act on customer requests. His visit made me rethink my opinion of the bosses and my perception of the organization. I'm not the only one. Most saw his visit as a major sign of recognition for us, who usually get so little consideration in the organization."

During our visit, we stopped by to see the vice-president. We told him his employees wished to see him more often in the workplace. His answer: "My schedule is full and I generally turn down all new meetings!" Our reply: "We know you're a busy man with a heavy workload. But don't you think you could find just a few hours, not tomorrow, but in a few weeks or months? After all, these people are putting in 2,000 hours of work for you each year. Don't you think you could give them two or three in return?" Our argument struck home and he agreed to the request. Our conversation ended with him saying: "You touched a chord—and that's what it took to convince me!" After spending some time with one call center employee, he publicly told the employees and managers he would be seeing them again regularly.

A few months later, we were leaving a meeting when we ran into the vice-president again and he asked to speak with us briefly. He said: "Two weeks ago, I went to a senior executive meeting at the head office. At this encounter, the CEO praised my regular visits with call centre staff, and cited them as a good example for other managers to follow with their own employees. I felt honoured and surprised by the impact of my simple initiative. You know, you were telling me there's always a payback for giving recognition. Well, that was one I wasn't at all expecting. Again, thanks for pointing out the 2,000 hours my employees put in!"

Just by taking interest in what people do, and asking them about their work, you go a long way in giving them recognition and making them feel important. Unfortunately, we are living in a day and age when employees have to ask for their boss to drop by. How many times have we heard an employee say: "He's never here!"; "He's just slipped out!"; "You need an appointment to see him, and the chances are 50-50 of it being cancelled!" How many times have we heard a manager say: "I don't have time to talk with my people!"; "I don't know what my employees are doing anymore!"; "I feel like a stranger when I get back to the office!"

The leading challenge to modern organizations is to increase the time that managers spend with their employees. A large metallurgy firm sought to remedy this problem through "leadership in action." Several plant directors decided that the managers should be on the floor, speaking with their work team for 90 minutes each morning. No managerial meetings were to be scheduled during that time. This single decision enriched communication between managers and their employees greatly, while improving labor relations and workplace safety. Something as simple as just being around matters as much as a strategic planning initiative, a five-year plan or a new organizational policy.

Just as simple and direct is recognition in the form of a few words of thanks. We recall a business trip we once made to London. During a free afternoon, we decided to visit the Tate Gallery. Like many travelers, we rode on the top level of a double-decker bus.

While we were contemplating the hectic London scene below, three teenagers boarded and promptly climbed up into our section. Barely in their seats, they began screaming, banging on the windows and hopping over the backs of their seats. We were alarmed but had no idea how to respond. Suddenly the bus stopped. The driver came up and told the youths to quiet down or get off. An altercation and shouting match quickly broke out between the driver and the youths. Then a police officer who happened to see the incident from the street got on the bus and helped the driver toss out the teens.

Peace was restored, but the passengers remained shaken. When we got to our stop, we went to the front and took time to thank our driver for what he had done. He replied that he felt worried because he heard a lot of noise and went upstairs without a second thought. We thanked him again and left the bus.

A few moments later, as we walked to the museum, the same bus stopped and its door opened. The driver we had just thanked raised his thumb in the air and said: "You made my day!" With a broad smile, we let him know that he had made ours too, and we continued on our way to the Tate Gallery.

We tell this story to show how recognition can be expressed simply and spontaneously to create a strong impact. Not only did the driver appreciate our thanks but by thanking us in return he helped reshape that unpleasant incident in our mind. By expressing our appreciation for his efforts, we also lowered our stress levels. When the driver pulled alongside to return our thanks, we received not only his recognition but also his assurance that we had done the right thing by speaking to him. His actions confirmed how important it is to offer simple, genuine and immediate recognition of deeds and actions we appreciate.

When we speak of recognition in the workplace, the first management practices that generally come to mind are results-based and monetary: productivity bonuses or profit-sharing plans. Such practices are common in many organizations. But how much impact do they actually have on employee well-being and business efficiency? The question is increasingly being raised. These practices have been around for over 20 years, and yet apparently have displayed few of their intended effects.

In his latest book, *Good to Great*,[1] Jim Collins shows that CEOs do not exhibit a direct relationship between the amount and form of their pay packages and their business performance. He also notes that senior executives are often paid less at companies classified as "great" performers than at mediocre ones. Apparently, monetary recognition is not the most effective way to boost performance. This is probably why 96 percent of Fortune

100 companies have nonmonetary recognition programs and why, according to a Mercer Human Resource Consulting study,[2] 38 percent of responding companies were planning to develop such programs further.

Since employee recognition has such a broad impact, we will take a few moments to define how it works. This is not a theoretical exercise but rather one of identifying the levers that are daily available to us in any organization.

> *Employee recognition is a constructive act of appreciation for a person's contribution, in terms of both work practices and personal investment. Recognition should be given formally and informally on a regular basis.*

## HOW TO DO IT?

Many studies and publications have focused on employee recognition practices.[3] Through our work and research, we have identified four ways to recognize people we work with:

1. Recognize the person's value
2. Recognize the quality of work
3. Recognize investment in work
4. Recognize results.

1. Recognize the person's value
   Here, we recognize the person and his/her distinct qualities, skills, know-how and qualifications. This recognition is expressed through interpersonal relations

23

and face-to-face encounters, and is the basis for all other forms of recognition. A few examples:

- Consulting a member of your team for advice and asking this person to attend an important meeting and express his/her views
- "Being" with your team and taking time to understand their work
- Publicly and privately emphasizing a person's positive attitude (either an employee or a manager).

2. Recognize the quality of work

Here, we recognize the quality of the job done, the ingenuity shown during the work process, the innovations that are suggested or the improvements that are continually made to a service. This recognition may include

- offering an employee an important assignment, based on ability and prior work
- presenting an award for professional conduct
- setting up a meeting to honor the contribution made by a group of employees to the organization (secretaries, accountants, engineers, etc.)
- congratulating an employee on a letter of thanks from a satisfied customer.

3. Recognize investment in work

Here, we recognize the involvement or contribution of an employee or team. Sometimes—and despite every effort—the results will not live up to expectations. You should still recognize the quality and intensity of the efforts, which are too often unseen:

- Honor contributions by backroom workers in such fields as tech support and administration
- Recognize the risks employees take to do their jobs, and the efforts they make

- Recognize the value of an employee's ideas, even when they fail to work out.
4. Recognize results

Here, we primarily recognize contributions by employees to strategic goals. This recognition is a judgment of an individual or team in terms of usefulness, output, productivity or performance. Such practices are widespread.

- Performance appraisal meeting
- Bonus for meeting a target
- Bonus for outstanding contribution
- Congratulations, during a staff meeting, on a success or achievement.

Recognition is not given only by words or acts that carry the label "Thanks!"; "Congratulations for a job well done!"; or "Keep up the great work!" It may also be expressed through simple management and work practices. People work each day. Therefore, you should as much as possible recognize their achievements on a daily basis. There is no need to be an expert in recognition to give recognition. Whether intended or not, we daily give it through actions, decisions and words. A senior executive increases a junior manager's spending authority. A team leader asks an employee to come along to see a customer because that employee has special expertise. A technician consults a worker to get a better idea of the sequence of production operations. An employee shows a young trainee how to perform a complex task. These are all examples of recognition. It is through this background of words and acts that we also acknowledge achievement. So be upfront and show your managers and employees how recognition may take different forms and is unthinkingly used by everyone.

People generally think of recognition as being aimed at someone. This is, indeed, its usual form. Nonetheless, during hundreds of discussions with employees and managers, we have often heard such remarks as: "Our department gets no recognition!"; "We, the technicians, get treated like a fifth wheel!"; "Secretaries don't count here, it's like they don't even exist!"

These comments refer to collective recognition and, above all, to lack of recognition of a trade, a group or a department. We must accordingly pay special attention to this collective aspect of recognition because teamwork has become so important and because cooperation among different departments is critical to success and efficiency. One such example comes to mind.

A large Canadian university organized a special seminar for the secretaries of its departments, faculties and services. Out of a total of about 600 secretaries, 563 signed up. It was an opportunity to thank the staff, with the university president and his management team greeting the guests as they arrived. A speech on recognition was delivered, followed by a workshop that offered a group experience of recognition. At the end of the day, each participant was handed a flower. The key message was: "The university works because you are here. Thank you!" The seminar, which was part of a broader strategy to instill a culture of recognition in the workplace, was greatly appreciated, as shown by these comments:

I feel privileged to have been present at such an event. This gives me a sense of belonging to the university. It encourages and motivates me to do my all!

We feel the university is making a big effort to promote recognition of its support employees. I think the university is on the right track to hold on to its staff and keep them happy.

I'm leaving filled with energy, motivated, upbeat and most of all focused on the key issue: give recognition!

This event proved so successful that other employee groups asked that similar events be organized for them. And so the past three years have seen five seminars of this kind, encompassing over 1500 employees.

Recognition is often an expression of satisfaction or gratitude. It can also be constructive feedback, a call to order or a request for adjustment. Remember, employee recognition is above all an honest judgment of a person or a job.

To be considered credible, and to have an impact, recognition must be used in proper proportion. You should know how to differentiate the good from the not so good, the adequate from the inadequate and the effective from the ineffective. We cannot recognize everyone in the same way.

While working with a nursing team at a large hospital, we were told by one nurse: "There are six of us in this unit. One does as little as possible and always has excuses for not doing the tough jobs. The head nurse does nothing to correct things! Tolerating this situation amounts to non-recognition. Do you think we feel like doing our jobs? No! Working a lot or a little makes no difference!"

By not acting and by not talking with the problem employee, the head nurse was guilty of not recognizing the other nurses. This kind of situation is not exceptional. We have all seen or heard of similar cases. To give recognition is not just to point out what is done right, but also (constructively) to point out what is done wrong, what has to be changed or what must stop. This kind of action makes the recognition seem more authentic, and also solves the unfairness of nonrecognition. To help the nurse and her team, we went to see the head nurse to talk about the situation, and there was a meeting with the unproductive employee, who was clearly told what her work entailed. The other members of the team told the head nurse how satisfied and grateful they were for this recognition of their problem.

As we have seen through the above examples, employee recognition is increasingly considered to be a useful management practice. Its many impacts and consequences, however, are still unclear to many organizations.

## RECOGNITION: A POWERFUL TOOL

Recognition catalyzes work performance. Just think of a five-year-old who shows a drawing to his mother. She asks: "What is it?"

"That's our house, with daddy, mommy, me and our dog," says the child.

"It's a very pretty drawing. We'll put it up on the fridge," she says smiling.

These few words were all her child needed to put his creativity to work, by papering first the refrigerator and then the walls with his drawings! "What a pretty picture!" Four words. That's all it took to stimulate the child's artistic imagination. As simple as this act of recognition might be, its effect was huge. Similarly, an employee or manager may just want a few words: "Thanks!"; "Congratulations!"; "By the way, you did a great job yesterday!"

Recognition also catalyzes health, giving energy and strength to pursue your work and the service you provide. We remember meeting a lineman when a major ice storm struck part of Quebec, causing power blackouts that lasted several weeks. He and his team had worked 16 hours nonstop. By the end of a hard day's work they managed to reestablish power to a residential area. With the return to normal, the residents rushed out of their homes and applauded the linemen. Spontaneously, and through a simple, warm and heartfelt gesture, they brought coffee, cake and hot soup. The lineman remembered how he felt, exhausted and worn out after 16 hours of work. "When the people left their homes to applaud us and offer food and drink, it was as if my batteries had just been recharged. We were ready to continue! Such marks of recognition are good for your morale!"

Just as recognition is a powerful way to mobilize people and build health, the opposite may be produced by lack of recognition. During interviews we conducted in the course of research on how people experience recognition, we had a chance to meet with a project manager of a large construction firm. She told us:

Last fall, my crew and I went all out to land a contract for the construction of a factory. It took us around five months of intense work. We wanted to get the contract. It was a unique opportunity that seldom came up. Unfortunately, another firm got the job. But not because our work was shoddy or our estimates overblown. The reason was quite simple. We have higher overheads because we're a big company—which isn't always a plus!

When we learned we'd lost the contract, my boss charged into my office to chew me out about how we'd let him down! I won't tell you the details of what he said. You know, people in the construction industry aren't always choirboys. When he left, I was shaken and furious. I swore neither my team nor I would ever make that kind of effort again. It's not worth the trouble!

As we talked, we began to understand the risk of giving recognition only for results, and not for investment of time and effort. In the case of this project manager, the work had been immense. True, the results did not live up to expectations, but the work had been done, and done well. The contract was lost because the competitor had put in a lower bid, and not because the work was of poor quality. The manager's boss, unfortunately, failed to recognize her efforts, being too concerned and perhaps rightly so, about the result or, in this case, the nonresult.

There was, in fact, a result. By not recognizing their investment of effort, and by unfairly criticizing their work, the boss demotivated the manager and her team. At the end of our conversation, she told us, "This whole business left me with a bitter aftertaste. I no longer see the company the same way. If you think now I'm going to invest myself in it to the same degree, you can forget it!"

Her last comment clearly sums up the dangers of non-recognition, and shows the moment when a rupture occurs between an organization and a person. The last we heard about this manager was that she had quit her job.

Another result of nonrecognition is that the person will turn to those who can give recognition. Sometimes, employees will turn their backs on a manager who has failed to recognize their contributions. Such employees will scoff at whatever he says or does. An unhealthy atmosphere, systematic negativism and ganging up by employees against their manager are seldom due to ill-intentioned employees. They are more often due to a bad work climate, which in turn is due to mutual nonrecognition between employees and managers. Providing such recognition helps to restore healthy and rewarding communication between the two parties.

Based on what we currently know about the relationship between human resources management and employee well-being, lack of recognition can have devastating effects on health, and in particular lead to cardiovascular disorders.[4] What accounts for this link? Whether we like it or not, work requires investment and effort. This daily personal investment results in an expenditure of energy that must be compensated for one way or another. Most people seek such compensation, and rightly so, in the workplace.

Such compensation is called employee recognition and, as with the lineman example, it is a positive health factor. It becomes a negative one when recognition is absent, as with the construction project manager. Health is thus built through positive relationships, and words with one's immediate employees and colleagues. Such is the power of employee recognition.

Just as lack of recognition has negative effects on physical health, it can also affect psychological health. Certain studies have shown that lack of recognition is the second-largest risk factor for psychological health, and that people who suffer lack of recognition at work are four times likelier to experience severe psychological distress.[5] Lack of recognition also affects behavior. A key

British study[6] points to a direct association between lack of recognition and increased absenteeism and alcohol consumption. This fact is well known beyond the realm of science and is regularly used in movies where a man, feeling unrecognized for what he has done, will drown his sorrows and not show up for work the next day.

Recognition also has a positive impact on those who give it, as we saw with the vice-president or the London bus driver. In fact, from all of our work with organizations, it appears that people who give employee recognition are felt to have strong social abilities and to be worthy of trust and loyalty. How many times have we heard someone say: "I'd really like to work for that manager. He appreciates the people he works with!"

In summary, recognition is key to motivation, to personal development, to positive relationships among people and to physical and mental health at work. It positively affects productivity and service quality, and it plays a significant role in the success and permanence of organizations. It gives meaning to a person's work and value to what he or she does. Employee recognition is, in a way, an indispensable companion for an individual and an organization.

## WHAT'S YOUR SITUATION?

Certain organizational conditions must be brought together to enhance success in introducing a culture of employee recognition. Based on our experience, the following practices stand out as the most decisive ones. By filling out the diagnostic chart, you will get a quick overview of how far your organization has developed a culture of recognition.

## DIAGNOSTIC CHART

| | |
|---|---|
| 100% | = We are often leaders in this practice—There is little room for improvement. |
| 80% | = We are leaders in this practice—There is some room for improvement. |
| 70% | = We are occasionally leaders in this practice—There is a fair degree of room for improvement. |
| 50% | = We are seldom leaders in this practice—There is a lot of room for improvement. |
| 30% | = We are not at all leaders in this practice—There is huge room for improvement. |

| | Leader, manager and worker practices | Score (%) |
|---|---|---|
| Leader Practices | 1. Senior executives define values, policies and guidelines on employee recognition clearly. | — |
| | 2. Senior executives are the first to take an active part in giving recognition. At such activities, their presence is strong and regular. | — |
| Manager Practices | 3. Managerial practices are clearly oriented to employee recognition (presence of managers, constructive and regular appraisal of employees, spontaneous acts of recognition, etc.). | — |
| | 4. These practices mainly involve recognizing investment in work (personal effort, personal contribution, etc.) and recognizing the person (positive attitude, ideas, etc.). | — |
| Worker Practices | 5. Employees regularly recognize the work done by coworkers. | — |
| | 6. Employees regularly recognize the work done by their managers. | — |

Once you have completed the company diagnosis, discuss it with the relevant people in your organization (board of directors, management committee, working group, etc.) to develop awareness of the importance of giving recognition in the workplace. The outcome of this discussion should help you plan and initiate the necessary changes.

# 10 Simple Actions

### 1. Conduct a survey on recognition

One of the first ways an organization can give recognition is to survey its employees and managers about their recognition practices, and how they wish to be recognized. Recognition should not be imposed. Consult your employees and get them involved in the decision-making process. That way, you will know their real needs are being met.

### 2. Raise awareness among managers and employees

To make recognition part of the organizational culture, you must make managers and employees realize its importance. Generally speaking, employees and managers do not measure how what they say and do will affect recognition in the workplace. This consciousness raising involves discussing the different forms of recognition, how to practice it, the positive and negative consequences and the obstacles to giving recognition in daily working life.

### 3. Make recognition one of the criteria used to assess managers

Everyone is for recognition in the workplace, just as everyone is for charities, but not everyone gives or recognizes!

The organization itself must see recognition as a desirable management practice. And managers should be assessed on this aspect of their job. If an organization wishes to introduce a culture of recognition into the workplace, it will also integrate it into the list of KPIs used to assess managers.

4. **Increase the presence of managers and executives**
   Increasingly, employees are asking to see their managers, and not vice versa. The managers, however, are often bogged down with the demands of their organization, and tend to work with higher-ups than with ordinary employees. Just by being around, managers recognize their employees, while also better understanding their work and spotting the many opportunities for giving recognition.

5. **Reduce the importance of galas and other ceremonies**
   Our surveys have shown that respondents above all wish to see more recognition of their efforts, their contributions and their positive attitude, with less emphasis on gifts, galas and ceremonies. These activities are often expensive and their impact is short-lived. In fact, what people want is simple, day-to-day recognition. It is better to take the money for a gala night and invest it in training or awareness workshops.

6. **Emphasize recognition in daily working life**
   To be fully effective, recognition should be given regularly and as often as possible. People have told us they would like to see recognition being given soon after the desired action or result. If an organization aims to introduce a culture of recognition, it will succeed only if such practices are part and parcel of the daily routine.

## 7. Disseminate information material

Recognition should be taught to managers and employees. It should be regularly discussed and backed up by supporting materials and seminars. Three strategies are needed: communicate, communicate and communicate!

## 8. Increase dialogue among the company's different units

Business processes are often represented by flow charts where everything seems to fit together perfectly. In reality, this is seldom true. Company departments tend to be unaware of what is going on upstream or downstream. They blame each other and communicate very little, each department considering itself to be the most important one and the least recognized. To introduce a culture of recognition, you should ensure that everyone better understands how the other departments work. Hold an internal get-together or seminar to show how each of them does its part, using concrete examples. You will thus help people better understand and better recognize each other.

## 9. Insist that employees give their managers recognition

Recognition is automatically seen as being a TOP-DOWN responsibility. Managers should recognize their employees. Although this is an important part of recognition, it is not the only one. Recognition is above all a human responsibility that is unrelated to job title. It should also be BOTTOM-UP. This principle should be clearly stated and discussed with your employees. They must fully understand and grasp that they will have an active role in creating a culture of recognition in their organization.

## 10. Discuss obstacles to recognition

Recognition involves things that may be simple, yet sometimes hard to do, for all kinds of reasons. You should discuss these obstacles, overcome any preconceptions, allay worries and provide ways to give recognition in daily working life. It is not enough to convince people of the need to practice recognition in the workplace. They must be willing and able.

---

### KEY POINTS

Recognition should not be an effect of work performance. It should be the cause.

- Give recognition every day in the workplace through simple management and work practices
- Be more "present" among your staff and employees, take an interest in what they do, ask questions to understand their work better—these things have a big impact on feelings of being recognized
- Increase the time that managers spend with their employees—a major challenge for our organizations
- Do not try to increase performance solely through pay and monetary incentives—these are not the best levers
- Show you have strong social abilities by giving recognition in the workplace. You will inspire trust, loyalty and desire to work
- Improve physical health by giving recognition and thereby boosting the energy and strength to do one's job

- Reestablish healthy and enriching communications between employees and managers by giving recognition
- Improve mental health by giving recognition. The risk of serious psychological distress is four times higher among those who do not get recognition at work
- Motivate others by giving recognition. This is a lever for personal development and a positive factor in human relationships. It positively affects productivity and service quality, and plays a big role in the success and long-term survival of organizations

# CHAPTER 3

# SUPPORT YOUR EMPLOYEES

During a field study among electricity linemen, we had a long discussion with a head lineman about the importance of mutual support among coworkers. This is how he summed up the role of social support in health, safety and business efficiency: "As a lineman, you have to work in a risky environment. There is the constant presence of electricity around you and the work high up on the utility poles. The work is always done in a team. You can't just think about your work. You have to talk, coordinate, cooperate, watch your colleague's work and advise him. To get all of these conditions in place, you have to rely on the other linemen, be on good terms, easily communicate with them and have known them for a long enough time. You have to always keep tabs on them and they must do the same for you. Once these conditions have been met, you're happy and your job goes beautifully!" Intrigued by his remarks, we pushed the conversation a bit further by asking whether he preferred working with a less experienced lineman or one who is more experienced but harder to get along with.

We asked because many organizations emphasize the "skills" of individuals. This criterion is of course essential, but often obscures the key importance of human relations within a work team. A team's effectiveness will depend on its members' expertise and, above all, on the ability to coordinate this expertise. Members can take turns to the extent that they know each other's skills. Despite the importance of work relations, organizations put less effort, fewer resources and less money into developing and consolidating work teams than into developing technical skills. For instance, most organizations have very detailed plans and programs on employee skill development. Employees and specialists will even be specifically assigned to define the skills of each job category. We know of no businesses, however, that provide the same framework (policies, guidelines, etc.) and the same resources for social relations within work teams. We need to strike a new balance between technical skills and healthy work relationships. Our experiences and discussions with many managers have clearly shown that a competent team is ineffective, and even a potential liability to the organization if its members are divided or communicate poorly with each other.

But let's get back to our conversation with the head lineman. When we asked him whether he would choose an experienced coworker over one he could get along with, he answered: "Without hesitation, I would choose the less experienced one. It's less dangerous to work with someone who knows less, than with someone you don't get along with. It only takes one screwup! Suppose you get into an argument with him and he decides he's not talking with you anymore and won't watch your work. You may be at serious risk, and he may not even see it. I won't take any chances! To stay alive and to do my job right, I'll choose the less competent guy. I'd rather show him the job, and even do a bit more work for awhile!"

This demonstrates the importance of human relationships and social support as key ingredients for well-being and business efficiency. Humans are social creatures. We need contact with other people, we need their recognition and we need their support. These three dimensions are not only job requisites but also factors for health and work quality when in sufficient supply, and risk factors when absent or wrongly used.

## WHAT IS SOCIAL SUPPORT?

Besides merely recommending that we develop social support, what levers does a business have at hand to encourage such development? Here, we will emphasize two levers that seem most important: instrumental support (task-oriented) and emotional support (person-oriented).

Instrumental support helps resolve problems encountered while doing the tasks we are assigned. As part of a pilot project on development of managerial skills, we saw the importance of social support and networks in problem resolution. The foremen at a steel-manufacturing company felt isolated. They had few opportunities to discuss their problems among themselves, few ways to take a step back and few chances to talk together. After a number of meetings, the foremen suggested they meet once a month over breakfast to discuss topics relating to the problems they experience. They did not want an agenda or seminars or priority issues for discussion. They wanted to have time to discuss their daily job. How should they manage the many adjustments that follow a change? How should a dispute between two employees be resolved? What strategy should they adopt to increase their budgets? How should they understand the latest supply guidelines? After several breakfast meetings, their comments were highly positive:

> We finally have a place where we can talk among ourselves, with no employees or boss around!

> I found very good advice on how to solve a problem that seemed to offer no way out!

> I never miss the meetings. They're better than coaching and less expensive!

This initiative clearly shows the importance of mutual support that leads to ideas, advice, help and courage to do a better job. Encouraging discussion and building relationships seem to matter, as much as designing a special foreman-training program.

Social support also promotes well-being and health at work by creating stable, positive social relationships—an emotional accompaniment that is positive, regular and person-centered. All of us experience trying times at work. A comment from a coworker may hurt us. A difficult discussion with a customer may leave a residue of tension. A company decision may run counter to our values. An employee's behavior may leave a bitter aftertaste. Usually, the first, healthy response is to talk it over with a colleague. Tell him about it and say how you felt. He will listen and may give advice. In both cases, the experience will do you good emotionally and help you get over the problem.

This kind of response is generally spontaneous. Not all of us have the resources to deal with everything that might happen in our personal or career lives. This is where individuals differ and where they can complement each other in coping with the sorts of happenstance we each must face.

Whether instrumental or emotional, social support may take four different forms:

1. Support from a social network
2. Support from a manager
3. Support for managers
4. Support from the organization.

1. Support from a social network

This support becomes concrete through different ties among people. A more or less solid social network may be a team, a collective, a trade union or a company department. These forms of being together create conditions for healthy workers and efficient work through positive and regular experiences, as well as stability and continuity. Their importance is summed up in a comment from one professor: "We form a great team. We get along well and mutual assistance is spontaneous. For me, each morning, it's a pleasure to see my colleagues. It's so important and stimulating!" A social network is also an excellent way to cushion the effects of a negative experience (by talking about your problems), to enhance a positive experience (by being congratulated on your success) and to counter any desires to quit, thus keeping job turnover low. If you tell your coworkers you want to quit, they will encourage you to stay, help you fix the problem or advise you on possible alternatives.

Generally speaking, a social network in a company will form within work teams and work groups. Unfortunately, today these teams and groups are in poor shape. In human resource departments, people increasingly speak of work group disintegration, of demotivated work teams, of the "We" losing ground to the "I" of individualism.

The problem is nailed down by this nurse: "Now it's everyone for themselves! We're so swamped we hardly even see our co-workers and don't know if they need a hand. You have to ask for help and it's embarrassing because it's the same for all of us, we're all overwhelmed. So we get by on our own, even if that occasionally means screwing up or wrenching your back! There should be more emphasis on teamwork!"

Many work environments suffer from this paradox: the pace of work picks up, staff are cut back and workers are suddenly told about the importance of relationships, cooperation and working together. Tension is clearly developing between production requirements and relationship requirements. We are exchanging a working world based on relationships for one based on transactions. By "transaction" we mean a workplace where information is exchanged and where you bargain through questions and answers, while never actually getting to know your workmates. To grasp the difference between relationship and transaction just think of the kind of dialogue you have in a store, in a restaurant or at some information office. This type of brief discussion is aimed at a specific point and does not touch us personally. And it is increasingly present in the workplace. It is like being next to, and not with, someone. So we need to set aside time after a meeting, at a meal or during a coffee break to talk with our colleagues and gear up to a "relationship mode."

Though important, a social network should be rounded out by good integration. It is not enough to have a team, a group or several colleagues you can rely on. You also need to be integrated into these networks, to have strong, lasting ties, and to share a history that stabilizes the teams and thereby ensures the quality of social support. Otherwise, support will be weak if the team has an unstable makeup, if its members are just passing through because they work part-time or on short-term contracts or if the work units are reorganized too often. Without going so far as to freeze everything, it is important to stabilize networks and work teams. This was the decision of a university hospital that consolidated its nursing staff by cutting back on part-time positions and by calling in the same replacement personnel, the aim being to maintain cohesion and to strengthen mutual assistance on the nursing teams.

## 2. Support from a manager

This support is key to social support. Managers are almost always considered by employees to be the representatives of the organization. They are the ones who direct and assess the work and the workers. Their practices and attitudes express not only their support for employees but also the support of the entire organization. We have often heard people tell us, "Here, the organization doesn't support us," only to realize, after a short discussion, that the employee was largely talking about his immediate supervisor. Too often, we confuse the terms "manager" and "organization." We extend our opinion of one manager to the whole organization.

When a manager helps his employees in times of trouble or when the work is especially tough, there is usually a feeling of being supported. Give people the resources they need to do a job, help them solve problems and advise, recognize and defend them—these are acts that show support for employees and their work. One of our friends is a regional manager of a financial service

45

firm. Just recently, he has been promoted to vice-president. This appointment can be put down to his professional skills, the performance of his regional office and also the excellent support he has given his colleagues and staff. The importance he gives to social support has made him a manager who can mobilize his troops. Undeniably, this has helped foster a climate of well-being and made his organization more effective.

For a manager, a supportive role does not mean passive management, or going along with all kinds of requests. Supporting your employees means using your decision-making power, for instance, by asking an employee to be less intolerant of certain coworkers or by telling an employee to put in a full workweek, like everyone else. At times, social support is shown through acts of recognition and compassion. At other times, you will be perceived as a source of support by showing authority and fairness.

3. Support for managers

Our research and actions in the workplace have shown us that support for managers is very often neglected. Indeed, it is easier to agree on the manager's duty to support his employees than on the organization's duty to support its managers.

During one assignment, to improve the working conditions of office employees in a major bank, the staff supervisors mentioned that they too needed this kind of help and that too often attention was focused on the employees and never on the managers. We tend to see managers as providers of social support while forgetting that they too need support. Many managers do not feel much support from management when the going gets tough.

In a chain of food distributors, where we were surveying the well-being of junior managers, the importance of this support came up regularly. One of them gave us the following example:

A few months ago, I had to suspend an employee for a week because I caught him napping in a corner of the warehouse. It wasn't his first warning and as far as I was concerned, he'd crossed the line. The next day, the labor relations office called me and said I had to give the guy his job back so as to avoid a long and costly grievance procedure. I couldn't believe my ears! I got zero support from the company, which went and overturned my decision without even a word to me! That was a bitter pill to swallow! How can I now get respect for my role as a manager?

A second manager told us about a problem he had with a customer over a returned bottle of wine:

Someone bought a fairly expensive bottle of wine here and then brought it back two days later, asking for a refund or an exchange. The bottle was two-thirds empty and the customer told me the wine was corky. When I sniffed what remained my suspicions were aroused. My warehouse assistant agreed: the wine in the bottle was not what we had sold the customer.

We asked the junior manager why this would happen. He told us that occasionally people would buy a bottle of wine, empty it out and replace it with a cheaper vintage so they can go back and get another in exchange. In this case, he refused to exchange the wine and the customer walked off with his two-thirds empty bottle.

But here is the rest of the story:

A few days later, I got a call from customer service, which had received a complaint from my customer. You won't believe what I'm about to tell you. They not only insisted I replace the bottle, but also offer my apologies as well. I was bowled over! My decision was simply ignored. Customer service never even saw the wine and took the side of that little con artist. Management ought to support our decisions. After all, we're the experts. There are limits to the idea that the customer is king!

These two examples show just how important it is to affirm and maintain constant support for junior management. The support should be concrete, not theoretical, and it must be part of your company's strategy. We encourage you to develop managerial support, action plans, resources and concrete tools that go beyond the simple slogan "We're always around if trouble starts!"

## 4. Support from the organization

A company is entitled to require a certain performance level from its employees, but it also has a duty to offer them its support. By fixing problems, eliminating risks, changing the work organization or offering flexible schedules, it proves its support and thereby improves employee well-being and efficiency.

Employees, technicians, managers and directors, all have their own opinions on the support they get and how much the organization is concerned about their well-being. A clear idea may be gleaned from the following comments:

> The bosses are alright with me. They regularly ask me how I'm doing, whether I've got everything I need, whether there are any problems. I get the feeling they think not only about their customers but also about their employees.
>
> (a secretary)

> Here, when you have a problem you can go and see the foreman. He'll do everything to help you. He's a great guy! Everyone wants to work for him. I consider myself lucky!
>
> (a plumber)

Company support exists when managers and management alike care about employees and their contribution and well-being. This concern shows itself in many ways. Here are a few:

- Be attuned to the needs of employees
- Give them what they need to get the job done
- Show approval for their decisions
- Give them recognition for their skills
- Allow for some flexibility in their work schedules
- Take action to improve their well-being
- Recognize the importance of their contributions.

## THE POWER OF SOCIAL SUPPORT

The four types of support we have just outlined show the power they may have over business, well-being and efficiency. Many studies have shown that individuals who have good support and are not isolated will get ill less often.[1] Social support also helps reduce stress, role conflicts and employee turnover. During our investigations, we found an interesting link between absenteeism and social support. When asked whether they ever showed up for work despite feeling sick, the respondents showed the importance of social support:

> Because I felt guilty staying home and didn't want my coworkers to be overloaded because of me.

> Because there was lots of work to do and if I didn't show up, my coworkers would have had to deal with it. And they already have plenty on their plates.

> I'm the only one in my group who normally provides the service and I didn't want the others to suffer the consequences.

> Out of a sense of professionalism and to avoid dumping work on to my associates. When I'm absent, they are the ones who replace me and they end up getting overloaded.

Beyond its effect on absenteeism, social support is also key to a strong organizational culture. If employees and managers do not help each other out, have trouble cooperating and communicate poorly or rarely, it is not only human relations that are affected but also the social dynamics.

This principle was understood by a manager at a furniture-manufacturing plant who felt that to motivate his personnel and ensure they comply with company goals he should create an open climate for discussion and cooperation. Here is how he put it: "If you want to motivate people and create a good climate for mutual assistance, you must focus on the people, speak to them directly, be present, help them, listen to them and encourage them to work as a team. By focusing on these factors, the rest will follow and that's what will make your business a top performer and its culture enjoyable." On a side note, this plant was the most productive of the six plants belonging to the company. The manager wound up our discussion by saying, "If you wish to motivate your staff, you should do it by managing people and not by managing numbers and files!"

In conclusion, the costs of improving social support are relatively modest. You should above all give more importance to interpersonal relations. There is no need for special equipment or very elaborate training beyond what is already available in many businesses. It is now up to you to provide social support with more time and space in your managerial practices. You will see how possible it is to improve employee well-being and business efficiency without resorting to sophisticated techniques.

## WHAT'S YOUR SITUATION?

Certain conditions need to be brought together to strengthen social support among employees and managers. Based on our experience, the most decisive practices are the following ones. By filling out this diagnostic chart, you will get a quick overview of social support in your organization.

## DIAGNOSTIC CHART

| 100% | = We often take the lead in this practice – There is room for improvement, but very little. |
|---|---|
| 80% | = We take the lead in this practice – There is some room for improvement. |
| 70 % | = We offer little leadership in this practice – We should improve. |
| 50% | = We are not leaders in this practice – There is clearly room for improvement. |
| 30% | = We are not at all leaders in this practice – There is a lot of room for improvement. |

| | Leader, manager and worker practices | Score (%) |
|---|---|---|
| Leader Practices | 1. Senior executives provide employees and managers with the tools they need to ensure their well-being on the job. | — |
| | 2. Senior executives provide employees and managers with the tools they need to meet their work targets. | — |
| Manager Practices | 3. Managers are concerned about maintaining a healthy climate of social relationships among the people they supervise. | — |
| | 4. Managers are given recognition for the support they give their employees. | — |
| Worker Practices | 5. Teams and groups are solid and provide people with substantial support. | — |
| | 6. Employees have a sense of belonging to their workplace and work with coworkers regularly without trouble. | — |

Once you have completed your company diagnosis, discuss it with the relevant people in your organization (board of directors, management committee, work group, team meeting, etc.) to highlight your specific action with respect to social support in your organization. These discussions will hopefully generate ideas and feedback that will certainly assist you in planning and initiating changes.

# 10 Simple Actions

### 1. Promote teamwork

We are told time and again: to be a top-rate company requires more and more effort. Success is no longer due to one person but to a team of people and their sense of teamwork. As a manager or employee, you must promote teamwork. Listen to others, be tolerant and help them out. Working in a team is a human quality, and also a winning managerial strategy. So make sure your team is in good shape, and not just "your machinery." Just as you should conduct preventive maintenance of your machines, you will also need to plan for preventive maintenance of relationships in your work teams through regular assessments and appropriate adjustments.

### 2. Share success and risk

Managers and employees must support each other in daily work life. Just as sharing of support means that success should be shared, it also means that risks should be shared. To be authentic, support must continue during times of trouble or failure. Avoid comments like: "I knew it wouldn't work! It's not my fault!" As a manager or employee, you should defend your coworkers from unjustified criticism.

### 3. Help your team become better than you

As a manager, you should not aim to be the best person on your team. You should aim to make your team the best, and better than you. To this end, encourage your employees, recognize them, support them, involve them in decision making and tell them you cannot succeed without them.

If you trust your capabilities and position, you can tell your employees they are better than you. By adopting such a view, you are not opening the door to potential dangers. Far from it. Your team will respond by showing you recognition and loyalty.

### 4. Forge natural helping networks

An individual may run into all kinds of problems that may come up at work or away from work. In either case, they will affect the individual's health and the organization's efficiency. They will often give off weak signals that are detectable only to close friends or relations. Managerial policies and tools are needed but are not enough, it being difficult to detect the problem soon enough. To pick up early-warning signs, informal requests for help or critical attitudes, you may create a network of natural helpers. Such people generally have a role of helping, listening to and referring people in trouble to specialists. Such networks exist in many unions, this being a model you might wish to use.

### 5. Set up a welcome program for new employees

When starting off in a job, people may feel a bit lost and lonely, often eating lunch by themselves. They have the impression of not belonging to the team yet. It is important to accompany new employees by offering them a welcome program and also a sponsor or mentor they may see if problems arise.

Such a program helps integration and shows there is real and concrete support in your business.

## 6. Encourage support and cooperation among teams

It goes without saying that cooperation on a team is key to binding individuals together and contributing to business well-being and efficiency. Yet most people will not automatically think likewise when the relations are between work teams or departments.

A person's well-being or a company's efficiency is attainable only through an ecological vision that integrates all of a company's components (team, unit, department).

Social support is not just up to an individual's immediate team. It must also be experienced within all components of an organization. Individuals, employees and managers must care about both intrateam and interteam relations.

## 7. Show loyalty

Social support is created and, more importantly, maintained when we have the feeling that we can rely on the people around us and that they will always be around to support us. Loyalty to your employees or to your managers is a key factor. This feeling is felt not only in your words but also in your actions. Talk regularly about the importance of the team, tell people around you that they can count on you and you can count on them. Explain the importance of showing loyalty.

## 8. Regularly hold team meetings

Team meetings are a very powerful management tool when properly used. They provide an opportunity for discussion and dialogue that allows people not only to exchange information and understand each other better but also to talk about their problems and seek advice from colleagues. Social support cannot be ordained. It cannot be imposed from above. It must be experienced through opportunities for face-to-face encounters. Team meetings are, in this sense, ready-made platforms for developing and bolstering social support.

9. **Increase encounters along the chain of command**
   We often hear the criticism that top management seldom mix and mingle with employees. Support must also be concretely shown by being present. Presence makes it possible to understand the work, to talk about what is going fine and what is not. By being physically present, senior management show their support to employees and also to junior and middle-level managers. These encounters are an opportunity for better understanding of each other's needs and expectations. Better understanding leads to better support.

10. **Make sure the individual has a network of social support**
    Whenever someone talks to you about problems at work, you should listen and give advice. Find out whether this person has access to a network of social support that may include colleagues, friends or family members. Having or not having such a network will tell you whether there is a serious lack of social support and whether he or she may have to cope alone. For the latter individuals, an employee assistance program might be worth looking into.

## KEY POINTS

- Social support comes about through emotional support, social integration, opportunities to feel useful and needed, confirmation of one's value and real, concrete help

- Organizations put much less effort, fewer resources and less money into developing and consolidating teams than into developing skills

- A social network is an excellent way to mitigate a negative experience or to enhance a positive one

- If work teams have high turnover or are reorganized too often, it will be harder to develop solid social support

- Give people the resources they need for their jobs, help them resolve their problems, recognize them and defend them. These are actions that clearly show support for people and achievement at work

- Managers are too often seen as providers of social support. They too need support. It is important to affirm and maintain constant support for your group of managers

- If employees and managers do not help each other out, if they have trouble cooperating, if they seldom or poorly communicate, it is not just human relations that are affected. It is also the organization's social dynamics

# CHAPTER 4

# DEVELOP A CULTURE OF RESPECT

Yes, we must live in harmony with our natural environment. But we must also live in harmony with our human environment.

—The authors

When we think about problems of respect and civility in workplaces, we all tend to imagine the worst situations—the ones that lead to ugly disputes, tense conflicts, acts of physical violence and even homicides. Such situations do exist and greatly affect workplaces. We must not, however, lose sight of the many other situations where lack of respect or incivility emits much weaker signals. These other situations include not saying "hello," showing scorn or ridicule, forgetting to say "thank you" or being bossy. These acts or attitudes of disrespect are legion, and represent around 20 percent of managers' work time. Beyond these figures, all of us can give examples of disrespect.

## DEFINE RESPECT IN THE WORKPLACE

The word "respect" means a lot of things, depending on whom you are, your age, your gender, your status, your culture or your religion. The Webster dictionary defines "respect" as "the special esteem or consideration in which one holds another person or thing." To get respect, people may be willing to fight, to protest, to go to court, to challenge, to negotiate or to die. The principle of respect contains two factors: show consideration (tact, politeness, civility or manners) and do no harm to others (do not harm, offend, upset or shock).

These two factors (show consideration and do no harm) underlay an oil company's decision in 2000 to confront lack of respect among its employees. Previously, many unfortunate events had been reported: frequent insults, discrimination, verbal abuse and even physical violence. The health service manager decided, with the help of a working group, to introduce a series of measures to counter these problems. An in-house survey found that over 39 percent of all respondents said they were regularly confronted with serious situations of lack of respect. Company management, on the recommendation of the working group, decided to act in several areas. A "respect policy" was adopted, and both employees and managers were offered training to help them deal with such situations. To raise awareness, employees also staged humorous sketches that portrayed common situations of disrespect. The short plays were presented several times in the cafeteria during lunch. The next year, the in-house survey was administered again and only 18 percent of all respondents said they regularly encountered lack of respect. Although the company's actions had not completely eradicated the problem, there had been an observable improvement. This example shows that it is possible, with willpower and effort, to act on the ethical dimensions of work, like respect.

This case is not unique. An increasing number of surveys[1] reveal that lack of respect has become a workplace plague. In a study of 775 employees by Steve Pearson,[2] 10 percent of all respondents said they had witnessed rudeness on a daily basis in the workplace, 20 percent said they were personally targets of incivility at work at least once a week and 78 percent of all managers had perceived an increase in incivility over the last ten years.

Disrespect is not serious only at work. Generally, our businesses mirror society. When we look at what is happening in our social environment, this issue clearly seems to be critical. Just think of the many reality shows such as *Survivor*, *Big Brother*, *The Weakest Link*, *Hell's Kitchen* and *The Apprentice*, where the goal is to eliminate your competitor, to break alliances and to humiliate the other person publicly. These TV shows are popular because they are based on conflict, humiliation and uninhibited anger, and in some cases, psychological aggression.

To counter this media-exploited trend, the British government decided to highlight the issue of respect. In 2006, Prime Minister Blair delivered a key speech in which he presented his "Give Respect, Get Respect" action plan. He defined respect "as a way of describing the possibilities of living in a community. It is consideration for others. It is my obligation to respect your fundamental rights. And your obligation to respect mine. These are our ties with society, and the agreements we maintain with others."

Issues of respect take many forms in the workplace. Here are a few comments we have gathered from our business surveys:

Management should show more respect for the areas of specialization of employees.

People should respect and recognize the quality and quantity of the work we do.

Treat people with respect. Ask simple questions: "How are you?" "May I help you?"

Encourage real listening and empathy to people and especially respect.

Work as a team and with mutual respect for the work of others.

Tell the truth and don't make false promises. If expectations aren't met, frustration will develop. Telling the truth is a sign of respect.

Employees and managers should respect each other.

As you can see, respect in the workplace does not mean the same thing to everyone, and expectations are not exactly the same. Let us take a few moments to define what we mean.

Simply put, "respect" is how we perceive behavior. It helps preserve mutually acceptable norms of civility on the job. It is a positive relationship with the other person, the aim being to forge lasting relationships and to encourage cooperation.

Respect is not a matter of status, prestige or social class. Everybody deserves to be respected and everybody should respect others, be they doctors, construction workers, company chairmen, artists, mechanics or even clergy. We remember a very big organization in professional services where we conducted a survey on employee well-being, including a series of questions on respect and psychological harassment. Were we surprised! Nearly one out of five respondents (18 percent) said they had suffered lack of civility. This finding had a major impact. No one expected that lack of respect would score such a high percentage among professionals. After questioning the results, this being normal when a survey's findings are at odds with client expectations, the CEO initiated a workshop on respect in the workplace, and said that he and his team would be the first ones to attend, since he was supposed to set an example. Nor was he never a victim. To develop a culture of respect, all organizational levels would have to attend. If some managers or employees considered their presence to be unnecessary, they could nonetheless help others grasp the importance of respect.

This is a short list of attitudes encouraged at the workshop:

- Treat coworkers with courtesy, politeness and kindness
- Encourage them to express their opinions and ideas
- Listen to what others have to say before giving your opinion, and do not interrupt
- Do not insult others or call them names or denigrate them
- Criticize constructively
- Recognize everyone's work and criticize less
- Treat others as you would like to be treated.

Unlike respect, lack of respect is a deviant behavior. It is often minor in scope and goes beyond the bounds of established social norms, in an organization or in a community, and leads to impoliteness, scorn, indifference or incivility to others. Harmless slights, verbal abuse or emotional neglect may leave people shaken and affect their daily life. Evidence of disrespect includes abusive language, insults, personal attacks, accusations, screaming, clenched fists and an overbearing posture.

These signs reveal not only tension among individuals but also may send signals of disrespect. Here are some other disrespectful behaviors:

- Acting as if you are the company's sole employee and speaking on behalf of everyone
- Failing to greet other employees
- Not saying please or thank you
- Refusing to put your effort into a group project
- Reading other people's e-mails
- Blaming a coworker for your own mistake
- Castigating someone in public
- Using coarse language in the workplace
- Raising your eyes when someone else speaks at a meeting
- Making inappropriate jokes
- Spreading rumors that may affect someone's reputation
- Talking on a mobile phone during a meeting.

By way of illustration, here is a real example of offensive words and acts collected in a study[3] on complaints of psychological harassment at work. To protect the person's identity, we have changed the workplace and his name.

## LUKE'S STORY

This incident occurred in a restaurant. Luke, who filed the grievance, was a cook who had lately moved to the area. The complaint was about one of his coworkers and his boss.

The restaurant could seat 60 or so people. It was a point of pride for the local inhabitants and the employees.

Luke was the head cook and a newcomer to the area. Coming from a large city, he had over a decade of restaurant experience under his belt. The owner dangled the possibility of becoming a part-owner if Luke could prove himself over the next six months.

At the restaurant, about ten people shared the hours of work. The waitresses were locally born and most had over three years of seniority. When Luke suggested hiring someone from outside the area to help him in his work, some of the employees, especially one, openly challenged his choice. The discontented employee had nothing good to say about the person and threatened to quit if the boss went along. The owner then suggested several times that he might break his promise and not make Luke part-owner.

Several days later, the cook noticed a radical change in behavior. His boss no longer had anything good to say about him, even criticizing the food he served. "Hey Luke, you're letting things go. The stuff you prepared is past the expiry date. I wouldn't serve it to anyone!" He also asked Luke to ignore how the waitresses and other employees were behaving toward him and to act as if things were going fine.

More serious skirmishes followed. One coworker threatened Luke: "You better watch it. You're the problem here and I'm gonna take care of you, you asshole. Believe me, it ain't over yet, if you think you can screw things up here for us!!"

A few days later, Luke, while looking for his utensils, seemed to think the same coworker had taken them. The coworker exploded: "Christ! You're not done accusing everyone else of taking your stuff? And it's not even

YOUR stuff!" At one point, his boss thought he was a drug pusher. Another employee called him an "ass-licker."

Luke had the impression these people were doing their utmost to make him quit. He could no longer stand being insulted but felt he had no real choice, having left the city to work in the restaurant.

How can we explain Luke's problems? Why did the work climate deteriorate to this point? When we examine the possible causes of disrespect, several factors emerge and several explanations converge. First, with more me-ism, less team spirit and cooler interpersonal relations, people think they can act and feel as they like toward other employees and their organization.

Heavier workloads are also playing a big role. People are always in a bigger hurry. We arrive late at meetings and do not bother to greet others so as not to disturb them. We step into a coworker's office without bothering to ask how things are going because we are concerned about our own urgent problems. We answer a customer brusquely because our work is still unfinished or we snap at a simple question because of fatigue. Unfortunately, there are not enough minutes in the working day and we often end up sacrificing basic rules of civility. There are also several other organizational factors that may cause an individual to lack respect for others. Here are a few:

■ Fewer and fewer jobs offer security (because of short-term contracts, outsourcing and an aging work-force), thus increasing the stress, making people more individualistic and less tolerant of others (looking out for number one)

- Organizational change may also be a source of tension among individuals (uncertainty, insecurity and fear)
- New technologies, such as e-mail, let you say things that may be regrettable because they are too spontaneous
- Managers may be good technical experts but lack the people skills needed for their position
- Casual banter between employees and managers may lead to impoliteness
- Too much of the workload provides too little time for people to explain themselves properly, and just enough for them to express (often poorly) their views
- Mutual indifference tends to degrade the work climate.

Disrespectful attitudes, behaviors and words may profoundly hurt a person's dignity, and even harm his/her physical or psychological health. They may also lead to detachment, disrupt relationships, degrade the work climate within a group of employees, generate disputes and reduce productivity. Indeed, we have found that victims of disrespectful behavior will focus more on personal self-interest and invest less in the organization. Lack of respect is often part of a vicious circle that may lead to psychological harassment.

## GIVE RESPECT IF YOU WANT RESPECT

If you want to be respected, start by giving respect. People will reciprocate if you greet them, ask about what is new, make sure they are comfortable with what you say, measure the impact of your words and avoid hurting people around you. Your relationship with another person will often be determined from the first contact, and the first impression will often set the tone for later dealings. We each have to find the way that suits us best. There is no One Best Way. Use "the way" that is most comfortable, and that will make you feel and look authentic. We knew a consultant who made a point of knowing people by name when hosting meetings. As he put it: "For me, using first names and speaking politely is my way of showing them I'm fully aware of their presence and that I thank them for being here. The participants get the feeling they are unique and not just 'The lady at the end of the table!' or 'The man in the corner!' For me, respect begins by recognizing the presence of other people!"

Despite all precautions, situations of disrespect may still occur. What happens then? Unfortunately, in many cases when a situation of incivility is mentioned to managers, their first response is one of denial and belittling. By different means and remarks, they will try to play down what happened. "You're exaggerating! It's nothing serious. Laugh a little! That's the way he is. It's no big deal. It's just a joke!" The second strategy is to put down the complainant, who is judged to be too sensitive (a thin-skinned person who takes offence at anything!) or who tends to exaggerate everything, and who "makes mountains out of molehills"! Several people told us that whenever they try to discuss what is going on, there seems to be no wish to listen or find out more. Instead, the response is to conceal and deny the situation so as to avoid the emotional ramifications, which divert attention from business goals: "I have enough problems with the garage. You're not going to bother me with all these trivial things!" Victims of disrespect suffer a two-fold pain: they feel insulted and are not taken seriously.

If the problem is not taken seriously, it will more likely happen again, there being no consequences for the troublemakers.

In most organizations, problems of respect are seldom of concern. If policies, guidelines or tools are available to managers, they are there just for extreme cases, such as psychological harassment, sexual harassment or acts of physical violence. Unfortunately, no such mechanism exists for less extreme situations, such as impoliteness, scorn, verbal abuse or malicious gossip.

Check out your own organization. Ask whether there are organizational mechanisms for dealing with problems of disrespect. We will bet you come up empty-handed. To get to the source of the problem, your organization should adopt managerial practices for situations that regularly come up in our work environments. Here are the most effective and simplest practices:

- See the presumed victim and, if need be, the witnesses. You need to find out their viewpoint and understand the work context in which the incident took place. Again, pay attention to the way people interpret the behavior they are denouncing before judging. Remember the subjective nature of the situation.
- Analyze the actions of the presumed instigators, find out how they explain the events and their behavior, and what may have motivated them. Unlike acts of vandalism or violence, where the intention to cause harm is more obvious, acts of disrespect are more subtly motivated. This ambiguity sets incivility apart from other cases of "bad treatment" in organizations, even though both imply lack of consideration for others.

It is essential to hear both sides. What is disrespectful to one person may not be so to another. Likewise, what is unacceptable in a company, a group or a work team is not always so in other situations. Here, culture plays a key role, as do personal experiences. Wherever disrespect is common, the tolerance level tends to be much higher—although this is not necessarily a good thing, far from it.

How should you develop respect as a key value in your organization? First, set an example. Show that respect for people is a fundamental value that ranks high among your company's core principles. At one of my talks, a manager spoke up about the importance of establishing respect as a central work value:

> We introduced a respect policy 18 months ago. For many people, it was just a scrap of paper and another policy that would gather dust on our shelves. I too shared the same opinion! But several months ago I had to deal with a serious situation of disrespect between two colleagues with the same rank in the company. Well, the policy enabled me not only to explain our position but also to require changes in behavior, not just because I wished it but also because it was now a company requirement and a condition of employment.

Since disrespectful acts often occur in private and target a single individual, it is important, as an individual, to respond quickly. Here are some responses you may consider:

- Do not accept intimidation, hostile attitudes, etc.
- Encourage victims to talk about situations of disrespect as a right, without fear of being punished for speaking out
- As a concerned party, try to temper reactions

- Apologize and explain if you have hurt or offended a colleague
- Assess how your own attitude and behavior may affect the conduct of other people
- Personally support anyone who has lived through a situation of disrespect
- Comply with the organization's official and unofficial codes of conduct
- Keep a situation from getting out of hand, and try to nip it in the bud if you are in a situation where disrespectful behavior is an irritant.

Your organization may also take concrete measures. Here are a few:

- Encourage victims to talk about disrespectful events and, as an organization, help them remedy the situation
- Deal with interpersonal conflicts, and keep problems from escalating within the organization
- Provide training about respect for both new and veteran employees and managers
- Offer courses on conflict resolution and communication
- Offer managers courses on ways to foresee and prevent violence, hostility and incivility
- Punish disrespect when and where it occurs
- Look out for warning signs
- Do not cover up for higher-ups who commit such acts
- Make employees aware of your code of conduct from the day they are hired
- Quickly and effectively respond to disputes or to any other situation at odds with the rules laid down by your organization
- Act discretely.

## WHAT'S YOUR SITUATION?

Introducing a culture of respect will depend on support from management, managerial practices and worker attitudes and behavior. Based on our experience, the most decisive practices are the following ones. By filling out this diagnostic tool, you will get a quick overview of the missing pieces you will need to help develop respect on the job.

## DIAGNOSTIC CHART

| |
|---|
| 100% = We often take the lead in this practice—There is room for improvement, but very little. |
| 80% = We take the lead in this practice—There is some room for improvement. |
| 70% = We offer little leadership in this practice— We should improve. |
| 50% = We are not leaders in this practice—There is clearly room for improvement. |
| 30% = We are not at all leaders in this practice— There is a lot of room for improvement. |

| | Leader, manager and worker practices | Score (%) |
|---|---|---|
| Leader Practices | 1. Senior executives provide guidelines on respect in the workplace and monitor the seriousness of the problem. | — |
| | 2. Senior executives practice what they preach in their leadership roles. | — |

(continued)

| | Leader, manager and worker practices | Score (%) |
|---|---|---|
| Manager Practices | 3. Managers have effective management tools (conflict resolution and discussion techniques, etc.) and adequate training to promote a respectful work environment. | — |
| | 4. Managers and specialized staff respond promptly when advised on situations involving serious disrespect. | — |
| Worker Practices | 5. Employees know how to recognize disrespect and know what means are available to resolve the situation. | — |
| | 6. Employees are not afraid to report a problem of disrespect they have experienced or witnessed. | — |

Once you have completed your company diagnosis, discuss with colleagues and/or senior management (board of directors, management committee, work group, team meeting, etc.) to develop awareness of the situation and to realize the importance of respect in the workplace. These discussions will generate ideas and feedback that will certainly assist you in planning and initiating changes.

# 10 Simple Actions

## 1. Draw the line

When it comes to respect, a line must be drawn between what is allowable and what is not. To show you are committed proactively, you need a credo or code of conduct that sets forth what kinds of behavior are expected within the organization. Since ethical issues are at stake, the credo must be discussed with and approved by everyone. After all, one of the first signs of respect is to ask people for their opinion before trying to impose specific behaviors, attitudes and ways of speaking.

2. **Set an example by creating a good atmosphere**
Your fellow workers will do what you do and not what you say. When we interact with other people, we either show them—or fail to show them—respect. At the end of your workday, ask yourself: did I act respectfully to the people I met today? Whether you are on a work team or a management committee, discuss the kinds of positive respectful behaviors that should be encouraged in daily working life.

3. **Help people understand the importance of respect**
When you feel respected, you are above all making a personal judgment that relies on criteria (which may vary from one person to the next) to interpret behaviors, attitudes or statements. So it is important to debate and openly discuss this issue and these criteria. It is also necessary to educate people, to assess differences in perception and to standardize perceptions of what is or is not acceptable. It is especially important to organize a structured workshop on respect and thereby provide an organized and relatively neutral framework for discussion.

4. **Define a procedure for settling cases**
A CEO cannot just say that he wants a respectful work environment and that he will not stand for any disrespectful conduct. An organization shows reasonable due

diligence when its words and policies are accompanied by concrete guidelines, procedures and management tools. Words are needed but are not enough in themselves. You also have to "walk the talk." Such procedures take many forms, and each organization must formulate its own procedure based on its characteristics.

## 5. Provide managerial tools for dealing with respect

A credo sets forth the framework for acceptable behavior. A case-management process provides a way to act in crisis situations. It is also necessary to provide managers with simple, fast and effective tools for early response. Such tools will enable them to respond before a crisis happens, being geared to solution seeking and nonthreatening to the parties concerned. The response may include not only disciplinary means but also, ideally, ways to find a constructive solution for everyone.

## 6. Survey/consult on respect

Before initiating any actions that will involve all members of the organization, you should take the pulse of the workplace. Survey the extent of the problem, its main manifestations, the people involved and the impact of any initiative. You may keep track of things by repeating the survey at later dates and presenting the data as a trend line.

## 7. Respond promptly

Whenever there is incivility or conflict, experience shows that "time never makes things better." Once a serious situation comes to your attention, deal with it. Action may take many different forms: referring to specialists, asking for a meeting with the people concerned, checking the facts, etc. What you must not do is deny, disavow, play things down or rush to accuse. A fairly simple method is to identify the points of conflict in the work teams and to undertake initiatives that are conducive to early resolution.

### 8. Ask for help
In cases of flagrant lack of respect, the inner wound may be so bad that one will initially respond by folding in on oneself, as with a stomach cramp. If the immediate need is for protection, the victim should talk about the problem quickly and seek help to resolve, and not just share, the problem. It is best to open up to people who will not only listen but also help find a solution. Although the first step is up to the individual, the organization has a responsibility to protect both the victim who is seeking assistance and those who will assist.

### 9. Develop tolerance
A workplace is always composed of people with different values, attitudes and practices that may vary. A work team or an organization should build on these differences and direct them to a common goal. By developing tolerance of others, we learn a key principle of respect: the respect of differences.

### 10. Give a second chance
Our acts may overtake our thoughts or lead to unintended consequences (pain, humiliation, shame). Or there may simply be a misunderstanding or error of communication. Although it is best to act swiftly, it is also important and wise to listen to the offender's viewpoint and give him a second chance. This approach is more conducive to resolving the problem at an early stage and to opening up discussion that will allow an exchange of views. Paradoxically, giving a second chance is also an act of respect.

## KEY POINTS

- Minor acts of disrespect greatly outnumber serious ones (harassment, violence, aggression)
- Two factors are present in the principle of respect: be considerate and do no harm to others
- Meaning of respect on the job differs from one person to the next, and the expectations are not exactly the same
- Everyone deserves respect and everyone should respect others
- Disrespect is a deviant form of behavior, often mild in intensity, that goes beyond the bounds of normal conduct
- When short of time, we often scrimp on the rules of basic civility
- If an individual is treated disrespectfully, he or she will focus more on personal interests and less on the organization
- Disrespectful behavior often leads to a reaction of denial or belittling, or to a judgment that the complainant is being too sensitive or thin skinned
- To be respected, you must first give respect
- Wherever disrespect is common, the tolerance level is much higher
- The first thing to do is to show that "respect for people" is a fundamental issue that ranks high on the company's list of core values

# CHAPTER 5

# RECONCILE WORK WITH PERSONAL LIFE

At the centre of any organisation, whatever its size, you will find its most important resource— the person.

—Patricia Hewitt, Secretary of
State for Trade and Industry, UK

Work has always been part of life, but for some time now it seems to be getting increasingly difficult to strike a healthy balance, and to mark the boundary between work and personal life. For many individuals, work has become their lives. Ask yourself: is it normal to devote more time and energy to work than to your family or your own needs? A 1999 Health Canada study states that 40 percent of all Canadians say they experience a high level of conflict between work and personal life, and that between 1977 and 1987 the rate of absenteeism due to personal or family problems had doubled. By 2007, the situation had hardly changed: 81 percent of all Canadians[1] hoped to strike a balance between work and personal life.

Today, work is being reconciled with personal life in many ways and is no longer something that only women call for. A very interesting study by a Canadian researcher[2] gives an excellent overview:

> A work-life conflict typically involves a job that encroaches on family life, a family life that invades the workplace and blocks advancement, domestic work that overlaps personal time or so much time invested in commuting that no energy is left for other pursuits. The conflict is ultimately between a person's different roles, with too much to do in too little time. Work-life conflicts involve constant time pressures. They mean contending with life on your own because you live with a workaholic or are the head of a single-parent family. They mean trying to balance your life with one or two jobs. They mean trying to strike a balance between life, education and work. Work-life conflicts mean putting off any plans to have children, or deciding not to have them (perhaps at all) because you can't imagine juggling any more responsibilities.

You may have noticed that we refer to "work-life reconciliation," rather than to "work-family reconciliation." There are many reasons why the first term is more appropriate. To begin with, not only has the workplace changed but so has the labor market. In the UK, Canada and the United States, single and childless people make up 40 percent of all workers.

Because of the new makeup of the labor force, businesses must accommodate not only families but also single people. Such individuals may have to care for parents with special health needs, they may be studying part-time or they may be involved in community projects.

In addition, what is needed is not so much "balance"—the word is little more than a platitude or a figure of speech—as "reconciliation," the fairest possible one between the needs of individuals and those of businesses. Such reconciliation must allow for individual and family realities, for competition and for the company's capacity to accommodate. It will never be perfect. The aim is not complete satisfaction, but rather a reciprocal agreement based on employee and company needs.

## RECONCILE WORK OR RECONCILE PERSONAL LIFE?

Which should be reconciled: work or personal life? In general, despite genuine improvement through company programs for a better balance between work and personal life, it is usually work that has prevailed over and dominated personal life.

Just one example: Try to invite a friend over for supper on a weeknight. Most likely he will tell you it is out of the question because he has to help the kids with their homework, clean up the house or is just too tired. The same may be true for you. Most likely, you would not invite anyone over for supper on a weeknight. You would not even feel comfortable doing so on a Friday and it would be out of the question on a Sunday, because you want to start off the week on the right foot. This leaves Saturday night—unless there is a supper with the grandparents or family members. This example shows just how hard it can be to reconcile work and personal life.

Hard does not mean impossible. If you wish to improve your possibilities of work-life reconciliation, there are three areas where you may seek accommodation:

1. Company support for you as an employee
2. Impacts on your career
3. Company demands over your work schedule.

Such accommodation should be tailored to each business, in line with its operational and service constraints, the gender of the employees and their family or personal responsibilities.

### What are the needs of employees and companies in work-life reconciliation?

Reconciling work with personal life must, from the start, be designed in both directions and not thought of as a one-way process. An employee is not a resource that is totally available to a company. Conversely, a company does not have to meet all of the personal needs of its employees. First, it must ensure as best as possible that an employee can fulfill family or personal responsibilities. Single parents will more often need leave from work to take care of their children. Some employees will have to care for aging parents. Others will need time off for a humanitarian cause they believe in. If a company can accommodate these needs, its employees will be healthier, more motivated and more productive.

In the other direction, your personal life must also allow your employer to meet its obligations. A company may serve the entire country and this means having employees who will work in outlying regions. Hospitals rely on nursing staff who will work during nights. A multinational company might need employees who will regularly move to other continents. Here too, accommodation can create gains in service quality, productivity and competetiveness.[3]

Work is reconciled with personal life through many situations that lead people to make choices. Will I work late and ask my mother to pick up the kids? Should I take my dad to the doctor? Can I skip work this morning to get my car fixed?

These situations are legion. To make decision making easier, one may try talking things over with the boss. We often would discuss such choices with our employees. In such situations, discussion would prevent conflicts between work and personal obligations, and our support helped achieve a win-win outcome for both parties.

We might add that our role in decision making has not been to tilt the balance away from personal life and toward work. Having lived through such situations ourselves, we know the solution comes from thinking through several criteria and alternatives. Our role, as managers, was essentially to encourage people to consider all work-related and personal parameters. In some cases, we postponed the work a few days, in others, the personal activity. In the overwhelming majority of situations, the employee was happy with the decision.

Work-life reconciliation means being flexible enough and having enough alternatives that you can get the job done outside the usual constraints. Generally, the constraints are due to time or space. When the issue is one of time, you may have to rearrange work schedules, vacation periods or holidays. When it is one of space, the workplace itself has to be rearranged. Beyond the specific details, the general idea is that employees can best reconcile the requirements of work with those of personal life by becoming more independent.

In a company or community, who can best step in and reconcile work with personal life?

The central role lies with each of us. Usually, we do not bother asking how important work is with respect to personal life when organizing our time or space. But the

83

question needs to be asked. Do we control our lives? This sort of introspection is often an opportunity to take stock, and make changes. This was the case with a management committee that was pondering work-life reconciliation and whether its members had to be available every night and weekend, even though the CEO did not impose this requirement on others or on himself. The managers and vice-presidents soon realized that they were overdoing things and that their duties were not an essential service that required being available around the clock. They turned down our suggestion to apply this management principle to themselves, but they agreed to pay more attention to the private space and time of their employees.

This short example shows that accommodation will be widespread if the consequences do not have too big an impact on one's career path. When talking with friends, especially women, you will almost always hear worries and remarks like: "I won't advance as fast in my career!"; "They'll ignore me for the big projects!"; or "I've opted for my family!"

Top management are not necessarily the level of management that is most open and favorable to work-life reconciliation. Presidents, vice-presidents and directors do not always have such a balance between their own work and personal lives. This is often how they have risen to the positions they now hold. So they have trouble understanding and accepting that what matters most to them, that is, work, does not necessarily matter most to everyone. They also have the means to pursue their ambitions. Their wives can stay home to care for the family or they may pay people to deal with their personal or family needs. Unfortunately, very few ordinary employees have the same means and have to cope by themselves with the demands of work and personal life. As one employee puts it:

> I don't have a husband to help take care of the kids and it's hard on my salary to pay for a babysitter in the evening. I can't get back to my work until the kids are asleep, the house in order and lunches made for the next day. By then, it's often 10 p.m.

Beyond certain corporate policies (e.g. flextime), work-life reconciliation takes shape on the job. This is where managers and supervisors have a key role in helping implement policy. Where companies support work-life reconciliation, managers are encouraged to back these measures, not to penalize employees who use them, and to step in when coworkers make disparaging comments. This kind of managerial support seems vital. Without it, the measures have less impact on people and organizations.

The bottom line is that policies and measures are not enough by themselves, and are much more effective when people feel that management is backing them. Managers should set an example, regularly speak about the measures and themselves have a balanced life. To help reconcile work with personal life, their managerial philosophy should be directed to achieving results and employee well-being. This does not mean that employees may manage the dynamics of reconciliation as they see fit. It is important to define how much leeway employees have, where they have leeway, the policy aims and the balance to be struck in each case. Both managers and employees gain by knowing what is possible and what is not.

Work-life reconciliation is generally thought of as a set of measures that apply solely within the company.

The community too, however, may also play a key role, one that companies should look into.

## How far should a company go in reconciling the needs of its employees with its own?

It is important to reconcile work with personal life, but there are limits. We suggest to the people who consult us that not all demands for accommodation should be met. We explain that the human resources department should not become a customer service that has to act on all requests. To guide your choice of solutions, we suggest the following criteria:

- Business impacts (cost/benefit). How will the proposed policy affect the product or service provided and what will be the costs and benefits to the company?
- What are the positive and negative impacts on customer service?
- Impacts on the work team and coworkers. How can employees and managers be encouraged to accept the proposed policy?
- What type of feedback have you received from employees and managers on the proposed policy?
- What problems might arise in implementing the policy?
- How could such problems be resolved?
- Can you recommend the policy to other units within your business or to other companies?

Once again, to avoid excesses, we suggest to companies and managers to set limits (guidelines, rules or measures) when trying to reconcile work with personal life. By doing so, you will not have to rearrange the organization of work to meet the demands of individuals. You will be arranging it to comply with the rules already spelled out.

## What are the obstacles to work-life reconciliation?

Although ever more workers, managers and organizations agree in principle that work and personal life should be better balanced, there are still major obstacles. One is excessive workload, lack of time to do what is requested and lack of human resources. Often, a company has just enough staff and usually even a bit less. There are also changes to work that are so frequent, or depend so much on customer demand, that it is hard to plan the workload in advance.

Furthermore, even if available, a work-life reconciliation program may not be easily accessible to all employees. For some, it may be bad for their careers. If a young team leader takes parental leave, as allowed by the law, he may advance more slowly or not at all within the organization. Of course, no one will say so openly. We have, however, met with enough management committees, managers and directors to know that, behind the scenes, this point will come up when talk turns to promoting this young man.

## WHAT'S YOUR SITUATION?

You should bring together certain conditions to ensure success when introducing a work-life reconciliation program. Based on our experience, the most decisive practices are the following ones. By filling out this simple diagnostic tool, you will get a quick overview of how far your organization has gone in developing a work-life reconciliation policy.

## DIAGNOSTIC CHART

100% = We often take the lead in this practice—There is room for improvement, but very little.

80% = We take the lead in this practice—There is some room for improvement.

70% = We offer little leadership in this practice—We should improve.

50% = We are not leaders in this practice—There is clearly room for improvement.

30% = We are not at all leaders in this practice—There is a lot of room for improvement.

| | Leader, manager and worker practices | Score (%) |
|---|---|---|
| Leader Practices | 1. The company has a work-life reconciliation policy that meets the needs of employees, clients and the organization. | — |
| | 2. Senior executives set an example when it comes to work-life reconciliation. | — |
| Manager Practices | 3. There are official management practices or mechanisms to help managers reconcile work with personal life. | — |
| | 4. Employees can use provisions for work-life reconciliation without suffering any adverse effects. | — |
| Worker Practices | 5. There are official and known mechanisms that people may use to report what they need for work-life reconciliation. | — |
| | 6. Employees feel free to avail themselves of work-life reconciliation. | — |

Once you have completed your company diagnosis, talk it over among people of your choosing (board of directors, management committee, work group, team meeting, etc.) to raise awareness of the situation and the importance of work-life reconciliation. These discussions will generate ideas and feedback that will certainly assist you in planning and initiating changes.

##  Simple Actions

1. **Avoid bringing work home**

   Some strategies are organizational in nature, others personal. You need to discipline your life, and control the balance between work and personal life. This balance requires a personal strategy to bring work home as seldom as possible. Leave your laptop at the office and put your BlackBerry in your desk drawer before going home.

2. **Cut communications with the office during vacation periods**

   Your holidays should be a time of total rest. When a jet engine is taken in for maintenance, the shutdown is total, like a horse at rest. This is also what most physicians will suggest. To recover, stop all activity. Since vacations are also periods for recovery, the same principles apply. Do not leave your phone number, do not let people call you and do not take a file home to read. In any event, you will not read it. Make a total break. Your recovery will be better and you will be more efficient when you get back to work.

### 3. Go home

A key to health is to keep control over your life and schedule. Know when to leave the office, when to have meals and when to take breaks. Set limits to work and stick to them. Try not to cancel personal activities for the sake of your job. Always question decisions to work late, to get up before dawn or to hold meetings over the weekend.

### 4. Negotiate your work conditions with your company

Empowerment is not just about controlling your work and having a say over how things are to be done. It is also about controlling or affecting the conditions of your work. If you have personal obligations, negotiate the accommodations to be made. Of course, not all options or wishes can be fulfilled. The company too has its own constraints and you must allow for them. But if your needs are essential to preserve your physical or mental balance or if your constraints are strong and personal, you should discuss them with your senior managers, and try to come to an arrangement that is suitable to both parties.

### 5. Create a more helpful work environment

Get your employees involved in developing initiatives that are suitable to all and advise them of policies and measures they can use to help them reconcile work with personal life. Encourage them to use existing policies and make sure they understand their careers will not be in jeopardy.

If some employees work irregular hours (evenings, nights or weekends), you can help them meet family or personal obligations by offering special services (day care, meal plans, housekeeping, etc.).

## 6. Develop a work-life reconciliation program

It is not just up to the individual to strike a balance between work and personal life. Nor is it the company's sole responsibility. This should be seen as a managerial issue—one of having guidelines, rules and procedures to manage an often delicate situation. An effective solution is to have a specific program to reconcile work with personal life.

## 7. Remember, overwork is bad for your health

An increasing number of studies have shown the link between too much time on the job and development of physical ailments, such as cardiovascular disease. This link should be made known to both management and employees.

Management should decide on

- number of working hours per week
- stand-by time of managers
- evening and weekend shifts
- number and duration of trips for company business.

All employees should each decide on

- the place of work in their lives
- their control over work constraints
- their ability to say "no"
- the state of their physical and mental health.

## 8. Work-life reconciliation is more than just about scheduling

With all of the changes going on in today's workplace, time on the job is no longer the only thing to be adjusted for better reconciliation between work and personal life. Electronic communication (e-mails, cell phones,

BlackBerrys) is also affecting the quality of time at home. Hermetic boundaries should be drawn between work and personal life, and not just for work schedules.

## 9. Promote informal support

Usually, when talk turns to ways to reconcile work with personal life, we immediately imagine specific guidelines, programs, rules and policies.

Less formal ways matter just as much in making possible accommodation easier. For instance, a manager should be sympathetic to employees who take maternity leave, and employees should accept the absence of a coworker who is struggling with personal problems. This attitudinal support is just as important as any official policy.

## 10. Support managers during implementation

The manager is always the one who must put into action the principles and directives of higher-ups. To reconcile work with personal life, managers will need support. Here are some tips:

- Create a bank of solutions that may be used as examples
- Go over specific cases with your managers to help them find possible alternatives
- Encourage and support managers who are willing to help out their colleagues.

### KEY POINTS

- Work-life reconciliation takes many forms and is no longer just a "women's issue"
- Because a growing proportion of people are single, programs should offer accommodations not only to families but also to the unmarried and childless

- You should be looking not for a balance but rather for a possible reconciliation between the needs of individuals and those of your company
- If a business wishes to reconcile work with personal life, it should help managers support such measures by not penalizing employees who use them and by acting when coworkers make disparaging remarks
- Employees cannot reconcile work with personal life as they see fit. Define what is possible and what is not
- When you accommodate one employee, you will inevitably affect the workloads, schedules, vacation times and duties of others
- Usually, work-life reconciliation is thought of as a set of measures that stops at the walls around a workplace. The community, however, may also play a significant role

# CHAPTER 6

# CONTROL THE WORKLOAD

Ever since my burnout, I've had two personal strategies for my workload. If my boss hands me an important file, I'll ask him to take back another file because now I know my limits. Other times, I just wait until he's asked me twice. It's incredible how often he simply forgets. Hah! Hah!

—An operations manager

In *Modern Times*, Charlie Chaplin depicted a worker totally submitted to the pace of production, as set by the factory boss. Does this story belong to the past? Apparently not. Today, workloads are getting heavier throughout the world. People report they are overwhelmed by work and lack the time to complete one or more tasks, projects or initiatives. The day is over before everything has been done, and we tell each other we need a little less work and far more employees. Our children are fed up seeing us work evenings and weekends.

Be it in the United States, Canada, Europe or Asia, many surveys come to the same finding: the amount of work per person is clearly on the rise. In 2002, 58 percent of American workers reported having to work relentlessly for their daily tasks, versus 25 percent in 1977! The latest survey conducted in 2000 by the European Foundation for the Improvement of Living and Working Conditions concluded that 56 percent of all European workers felt they were working at a frantic pace and 60 percent had very tight deadlines. Our surveys also show that 55 percent of all Quebec employees think they work under severe time constraints. This widespread intensification of work has impacts on health, with 24 percent of all workers feeling always or almost always generally tired. Fatigue has major economic impacts. A recent study on the US labor force[1] revealed that workers with symptoms of fatigue annually cost employers $136.4 billion in lost time, versus $101 billion for workers with no such symptoms.

All of the world's labor experts (economists, sociologists, physicians, psychologists, etc.) agree that over the past 20 years, the amount of work has increased, the time to do it has shortened, the planning process has been cut back and products and services have diversified almost beyond limit. Meanwhile, work is also being constrained by concerns over quality, security and safety and by shorter lead times between ordering and delivery. The rising amount, pace and constraints of work are closely linked to the demands of being globally competitive, meeting customer requests, pleasing shareholders and developing production methods that aim for higher business efficiency. To quote Laïdi's book *La tyrannie de l'urgence*, we are living in a world where urgency is overloading our working hours with demands that exist only in the here and now.

The quest for efficiency does not always mean improved employee well-being. As a pharmaceutical plant operator told us: "We introduced a Kaizen (continual improvement) program in our bottling section. We moved the equipment closer together and brought back part of the maintenance service, which had been on the other side of the plant. A few weeks after the new workstation layout, many of us noticed we had much less time to relax and catch our breath. Previously, we had to wait for the maintenance technician. Now, he's right next to us. That doesn't seem like a lot, but we miss the 45-second wait time we used to have several times a day! Frankly, at the end of the day, I feel more tired!" The Kaizen changes certainly helped speed up production, but at the cost of making everyone work harder and longer, with no rest periods. The effects were positive on production but negative on employee well-being!

At the same time that new approaches are being taken to reengineer production or service processes, businesses have long ceased to assess employee and manager workloads. During a survey on work-related stress in three major private and public organizations, we asked managers how workload was managed, whether they had methods, tools, guidelines or procedures to adjust what was being asked of employees to what they could do. In every case, nothing was available. The answer was always: "We don't have any specific tool or method, but if people have too much, they can come and talk."

Today, one of the few workload factors to be assessed is the physical dimension. Ergonomists, engineers and physicians measure physical exertion on the job with dynamometers, electrocardiograms and heart rate or blood pressure devices. With these tools, they have managed to reduce some of the laboriousness of work. Just think of the systems for handling heavy loads, the ergonomic layouts of workstations or the automation of tasks that require unhealthy postures. The changes have been considerable and have made work less laborious. But the workload issue has not been fully settled yet.

While there are tools to measure laboriousness, there is no equivalent to measure the more virtual demands of work (concentration, vigilance, speed, multitasking, complexity, impact of decisions, surveillance, etc.). For this, we do not solely blame the organizations, engineering firms or human resource departments. We also blame the specialists in work organization, in management and in industrial psychology who put forward very few tools or methods for work assessment. Indeed, what tools are available to measure the workload of a manager, a social worker, an engineer or a computer programmer? Oh, of course, one may count how many employees work under a manager's supervision, how many homes a social worker has to visit, how big an engineer's project is or how many changes a programmer has to make to a program. But that is not representative of all the demands of work! The manager's workload will not be the same if his employees are in different regions, the social worker's workload will depend on the seriousness of the cases to be visited, the engineer's workload will hinge on the number of subcontractors and the programmer's workload will reflect the speed of the computer network and hardware available. As we may already begin to realize, workload is not merely a matter of how much work has to be done.

But what does it mean to be overloaded, to be short of time, to have to work too fast, to be unable to get any rest? When we ask our colleagues how things are going we get the same answer 99 percent of the time: "I'm swamped!"; "It never stops!"; "I have no idea when I'll finish!" With these comments, they are saying they are overloaded. But what is a normal workload? In the next few paragraphs, we will explore what this term really means.

## A NEW VISION OF WORKLOAD

Traditionally, workload has been defined as the amount of work to be done, as the limit to physical labor and as the limit to cognitive processing of information. The word "load" itself evokes the weight and amount of work. Today, in the twenty-first century, this is no longer the case.

We are moving from an industrial economy to a service economy. Some work is still physical (lifting, drawing, pushing) but most is intellectual (analyzing, describing, inspecting, supervising, etc.). It is less concrete (tons of coal to be shipped, number of cars to be made, distance to be traveled) and more virtual (quality of the service, accuracy of the reply, satisfaction of the customer). With these many changes to businesses and to work, we should redefine "workload" to cover all factors, whether old or new, that impact on the well-being of people and on business efficiency. We propose three components of a more up-to-date definition of workload:[2]

1. What is asked for
2. What is felt
3. What is actually done.

1. What is asked for
This first component of workload, **what is asked for**, corresponds to the production requirements. It encompasses quantitative performance goals (i.e., number, duration, magnitude) and qualitative ones (i.e., satisfaction, trust, reputation, loyalty). This component is the visible side of work—what is written in job descriptions, productivity goals, assignment definitions or improvement plans.

But what is asked for is not always what is done. Jobs evolve quickly. Yesterday's workday is not the same as today's, and today's will differ from tomorrow's.

The complexity of work was described to us by an account manager. Carole works at a major financial institution, where she has been an account manager for the past two years. She loves the job and gives it her all. Her customers are pleased and her coworkers are delighted by her dynamism and availability. But for three months now, it seems to her that she has been the one often stuck with new assignments, and she is now asking herself questions because her customer service is paying the price. Recently, her boss asked her to take on a computerization project. She said yes half-heartedly, wondering how she could do it. Working nights? Taking shorter lunches? No longer talking with colleagues? There was no clear way. Her boss seemed surprised by her rather lukewarm response but said nothing.

We asked Carole what her job was. She answered: "account manager." We replied: "No, that's your job title. We want to know what you do every day." Laughing, she answered: "I hope you have time because it's going to be long!" After two hours of talking, we had a list of 35 different activities, assignments, projects, committees or responsibilities. We also found out that many of the activities were regularly interrupted, carried out simultaneously or had the same deadlines. Workload is thus not just the amount of activities but also the multitasking and scheduling conflicts they entail: meetings at the same time, same-day delivery deadlines or same-day answers that require the same kind of extra work.

Realizing just how much work she was doing, she told us: "I never thought I was doing so much. I had no idea, but I was feeling the effects! I better understand now why I feel exhausted at the end of my workdays. I used to think it was my age!" She had never taken time to analyze her work, to take stock of her tasks, to list the committees or to add up the number of times she had been asked to help a coworker. Carole had no overall vision, and neither did her boss and colleagues.

At the end of our talk, we suggested that Carole clean up her list, group her activities by category (meetings, customer visits, consultations, etc.) and sit down with her boss to talk it all over. We saw Carole again a few weeks later. She had indeed talked with her boss, who was surprised by the amount of work she had and agreed it was far too much. Her boss commented that he did not want to lose someone with Carole's potential as an account manager. Together they agreed to take her off a few committees and two assignments that had been demanding much of her time. The solution was a real relief for Carole. She felt as if she had taken back control of her work and could continue to offer her customers quality service. A bit later, we suggested to her boss that he take the same approach with all his employees. We suspected Carole was not the only one with too much work. In addition to improving employee well-being, he would also be boosting efficiency and productivity within the department. Good economic performance is, in fact, linked to a reasonable workload and a pace of production within the range of human ability. Less work per person does not mean lower company earnings.

All of us see "workload" as something we have to do, but it is more than just what ends up getting done. In other words, it also includes unfinished, abandoned and failed attempts. These concealed aspects—what we might call "shadow work"—hang in the balance and often contribute a lot to the feeling of being overloaded.

## 2. What is felt

To define "workload," we should not simply identify what is asked for. We should also question the employees about what they feel, while remembering that workload does not affect everyone the same way. For the same job, one person will feel overloaded and the other just fine. Who is wrong and who is right? In an organization, the one who is wrong is supposedly the one who complains. Is this really true?

The following example will show how you can deal with your workload by changing working conditions, as discussed in the last section, and also by dealing with the individual.

One day, an airplane mechanic told us he felt stressed out and exhausted by his job. For the past two months, he had been manufacturing gear assemblies with a new high-precision machine. The precision had to be within a thousandth of an inch. He told us: "At the end of each working day I'm beat. I have trouble concentrating and I'm afraid of slipping up!" During our conversation, we learned he had not been fully trained to operate such a machine. An employee had explained to him what to do one morning, but that was it. The rest was trial and error. He himself admitted that the amount of work was reasonable, but he did not feel proficient. He was in constant fear of making a mistake, wasting costly parts and getting reprimanded by his supervisor. In this case, the solution was not to reduce his workload or to provide an assistant who could help him meet the production goals. The solution was to develop his skills and expertise.

Had we not been interested in this worker, in what he felt in relation to what he had to do, we would have inaccurately diagnosed his workload problems. Had he gone to see his supervisor and simply said, "I've got too much work," the man would have looked around and replied: "You're doing the same job as the others and yet your production is lower. Where's the problem? I don't see any!" He would have gone back to his workstation feeling unhappy, misunderstood and with no solution in sight.

What actually happened was quite different. After our meeting, the mechanic went to see his supervisor and explained the stress he was experiencing. We advised him to state right away that the problem was not the amount of work, so that his supervisor would not become dismissive and closed-minded. He described his deficiencies, what he called his "skill gaps" and asked for a few days of coaching with a more experienced employee to help him overcome his difficulties. His supervisor was very receptive and the requested support was provided the next week.

Now back to our analysis of workload. During our action research on work-related stress, we noticed a perverse effect—a vicious circle of overwork. When a working group was being set up at a city hall, it was difficult to find managers who wanted to or could sit on a work-stress reduction committee. The few who agreed wished to improve both the employees' situation and their own. Nonetheless it was very hard to get them to attend each meeting. There were different reasons: an urgent meeting, a discussion with the CEO, last-minute problems and so on. While meeting with researchers involved in this project, we remarked that the managers' workload was keeping them from fixing the workload problem. The paradox was confirmed by the other researchers there, who mentioned similar situations. Thus, overwork hurts not only well-being and efficiency but also efforts to trim it back. When employees and managers are overloaded, they do not even have time to care for their well-being. They can only grin and bear it.

So when we define workload, allowance should be made for what individuals feel toward their own workload. This subjective experience may be interpreted positively as career enrichment or negatively through various effects: psychological distress, worry, constant uncertainty, demotivation, exhaustion or irritability.

3. What is actually done

Workload may be understood as an equation: what the company asks for + what the worker feels. We must consider both components to act effectively. Otherwise, pieces will be missing when we define the amount of work an employee should do. This equation is commonly used among production engineers. To define a production process, they will estimate how many operations are performed, the number of mechanical arm movements, the torsions in hydraulic lines or the demand for energy. They will also estimate the effects on equipment (what is felt, if I may say, by the machine): pressure on mechanical seals, tensions on hydraulic lines, corrosion of weld points and many other mechanical, electrical or chemical parameters.

This kind of calculation—estimating what is asked for and what is felt—is regularly performed in a business environment. It is not a new process in operations management. What is new is the target of assessment, which should be expanded beyond industrial equipment to include humans. We need to confront two questions: (1) what is being asked of this human? and (2) what does he or she feel?

Using both questions, here is how we could analyze the work of a grocery store manager.

First, what are the store managers asked to do? Here are a few of their duties, as defined by the organization:

- Supervise and coordinate the staff
- Ensure the quality of customer service
- Manage the store's budget, sales and operations
- Control inventories and supplies
- Oversee the marketing and merchandising plans for products and services.

Now, what do they say when they talk about their work?

We aren't trained to handle interpersonal conflicts.

Developing outside markets (through stands at festivals, fairs, special festivities, etc.) comes on top of our regular activities and leaves us with less time for the store. So we have to return late at night to prepare for the next day.

It's hard to take time off, because we don't have any assistant managers. The most senior employee manages the store if we're away. Even so, we tend to drop in and check to see that everything is OK or rush back from a day off to make sure no problems happened in our absence.

The daily routine is so time-consuming that I haven't any time to develop my own technical skills to properly use the new computer system. It takes up all our time.

The actual workload is thus a combination of what is asked for and what is experienced or felt by the managers. Usually, neither is assessed. Our investigations have led us to ask three different organizations whether they assess their workloads. In each case, the answer was "no." We were told that employees could come and talk about their workload at any time. As we have already pointed out, this means the workload was not being managed. When you manage an activity, you have management tools, guidelines, policies or criteria. That was not so in any of the three organizations.

## WHAT'S YOUR SITUATION?

Workload is key to employee well-being and business efficiency. You should carefully find out whether all conditions are in place for better workload management. Fill out this diagnostic tool to get a quick overview of the main actions needed to manage employee and manager workload.

## DIAGNOSTIC CHART

| | |
|---|---|
| 100% | = We often take the lead in this practice—There is room for improvement, but very little. |
| 80% | = We take the lead in this practice—There is some room for improvement. |
| 70% | = We offer little leadership in this practice—We should improve. |
| 50% | = We are not leaders in this practice—There is clearly room for improvement. |
| 30% | = We are not at all leaders in this practice—There is a lot of room for improvement. |

| | Leader, manager and worker practices | Score (%) |
|---|---|---|
| Leader Practices | 1. Senior executives have set guidelines for management of employee workloads. | — |
| Leader Practices | 2. Manager workloads have been assessed so that managers can spend more time with their employees. | — |
| Manager Practices | 3. There are tools for measuring employee workloads (task analysis, performance appraisal, etc.), when new tasks are assigned. | — |
| Manager Practices | 4. Managers take concrete action to reduce employee workloads. | — |
| Worker Practices | 5. Employees feel free to speak about their workloads with their supervisors. | — |
| Worker Practices | 6. Employees can seek and get help if they feel overworked. | — |

Once you have completed your company diagnosis, talk it over among people of your choosing (board of directors, management committee, work group, team meeting, etc.) to develop action plans aimed at dealing with employee workload. These discussions will generate ideas and feedback that will certainly assist you in planning and initiating changes.

# **10** Simple Actions

## 1. Assess the actual workload

To measure an employee's workload, look at two components.

First, identify what is being asked for (amount, deadlines, intensity, pace of work). You should review job descriptions, consult production or productivity reports and discuss goals with managers.

Next, analyze the work that is actually being done and experienced, and identify what has been left out from the previous phase of analysis. Pay special attention to extra duties, level of difficulty, wait times, lack of coordination with other job positions, interruptions, delayed tasks, etc.

These two components should be the basis for discussing a person's workload, and not simply the job description.

## 2. Just say NO!

Just turn down a request to attend a meeting or to change your job goals. You will be better able to finish an assignment on schedule, to devote more time to your customers or to avoid being late for a meeting. Saying "no" is often the best way to break the vicious circle and win the race against time. You should be bossing time around, and not vice versa!

Be sure to justify your response. Explain that your refusal is motivated by a desire to finish a job properly and not be late. These are qualities that others will recognize and appreciate.

## 3. Reduce the workloads of your managers

Managers have continually increasing workloads and may have trouble saying "no" to what they are asked to do.

This overwork is harmful to their well-being, to their relationships with their employees and to the proper functioning of their organization. The solutions are simple but courageous:

- Establish a quota of committees or working groups for each manager
- Set aside periods of the workday when no meetings will be allowed, in order to free up time and enable managers to spend more time with their employees
- Reassess the appropriateness of administrative reports
- Scale back or postpone organizational projects.

## 4. Add staff

There are times when you cannot do more with less. Organizations have cut back massively in recent years and work itself involves more constraints. Clearly, in some cases, the solution is to take on more staff.

This situation is not just the lot of employees. Managers too are overwhelmed. The span of control is often too great, that is, the employee/manager ratio is too high.

It is thus essential to document, with facts and figures, the need to open up more job positions or to find replacements for managers who are away.

## 5. Draw up a "Not to do" list

In our culture of efficiency, urgency and quantity, we have developed a number of tools to manage our time and priorities. The best example is the "To do" list. Such tools are useful because they help us organize our workload (or overload). But they also entrap us by constantly adding another little task, an idea that may be interesting, a new project and so on. Paradoxically, these work organizers are excellent ways to increase our workloads.

To reduce your workload, make a "Not to do" list. Your "Not to do" list should be an opportunity to identify the items of your actual work that do not fall within your purview. Here are a few to start off your list:

- Clarify and be aware of your role and duties
- Delegate administrative work
- Identify tasks that consume much of your time.

6. **Talk with others about what they feel on the job**
   Workload is not simply a matter of quantity. More and more aspects of workload are invisible and indeed virtual. They include the complexity, accuracy, quality or subtlety of actions to be taken or decisions to be made. It is essential to talk with employees to find out this hidden side of workload. To improve their well-being and your company's efficiency, you should look into what they feel when going about their jobs.

7. **Get employees involved in defining their workloads**
   Workload is not just a matter of quantity. Therefore, reducing it is not the whole solution. An important step is to consult the people who say they are being overworked.

   So dealing with workload is more than just lessening it. You must also help your employees define the problem. This strategy is effective because it provides an opportunity to define what has to be done and to adjust and perhaps reduce the workload. In fact, people will more readily accept what they have to do and the amount of work to be done once they have a chance to give their opinion.

8. **Cut down on interruptions**
   Workload is not just the amount of work to be done, but also the way it is done. One serious impediment to work is interruption. It is a major source of irritation and may

take different forms: e-mails, phone calls, impromptu visits, etc.

Here are a few ways to limit its impact:

- Close your e-mail inbox to stay concentrated
- Answer your messages in one batch and not one by one. Set aside a period for this activity in the late morning or late afternoon
- Do not answer the phone if you have to finish an assignment with a tight deadline.

9. **Set aside time for your return from vacation**

   How often have we heard people say they are penalized for taking time off with huge piles of work waiting when they return?

   Develop the following strategy. Leave a message on your voicemail saying that you are coming back two days later than you actually will. That leaves enough time to catch up. Try to dodge phone calls during those two days. This does not eliminate the whole backlog, but it does cushion the shock of coming back and helps preserve some of the beneficial effects of our holidays.

10. **Turn down additional work when the team is already overwhelmed**

    Workload is not assigned solely on an individual basis. Often, the work team as a whole has to deal with new assignments, projects and deadlines. In this, managers have a key role. They must avoid overloading their staff to the point of almost inevitably causing problems in production, service or work climate.

    Protect your staff and ensure that the required or imposed workload can be done under conditions that will not undermine employee well-being and company efficiency.

## KEY POINTS

- All world specialists agree that work has greatly intensified over the last 20 years
- Organizations are suffering from a decrease in the quantity and quality of products and services because the increase in the workload is hindering the initiative and creativity of employees and managers
- Most organizations lack adequate management tools to assess the workloads of their employees and managers
- Workload has three components: what is asked for, what is felt and what is actually done
- Workload also includes what is not done, what has not been finished, what has been abandoned and what has been tried but to no avail
- Lighter workloads do not mean lower corporate earnings
- Overloaded employees and managers do not even have time to care for their own well-being
- In saying they are overloaded, employees and managers do not necessarily mean they wish to work less

# CHAPTER 7

# ENCOURAGE AND SUPPORT AUTONOMY AND PARTICIPATION IN DECISION MAKING

From our work in the field, autonomy and participative decision making come up as a core positive aspect of work, as this marketing executive reflects.

> I have 15 years of experience as a marketing specialist. I've had to deal with big clients and multi-million dollar ad campaigns. My expertise was recognized by my former boss. Since the new one arrived, I'm less and less involved in decision making and I have to check my decisions with my boss. I have the impression of being poorly used and that he sees me as a threat. For me, my autonomy is essential and I also know I've got the skills needed for our department's goals. If things don't get better, I'm going to ask for a transfer!

This situation has two major aspects: (1) autonomy and (2) participation in decision making. We regularly hear this sort of comment from the people we meet. They wish to take part in organizing their work and in developing the future course of their team. This wish is an important one. Only 56 percent of all employees who answered our surveys stated that their immediate supervisor encouraged them to take part in major decisions. Let us be clear. Employees do not want power. They want to participate, to be informed, to be consulted and to take part in defining their work. This wish is not motivated by a desire to control other people or things, but by a desire to offer their expertise in organizing their own work or in making company decisions. Through autonomy and participation in decision making, people can know and affirm their role in the organization. This possibility and ability to influence is key to employee well-being and business efficiency. In a recent French study, the researchers[1] found that 41.5 percent of all people questioned valued first and foremost self-expression in their work and the use of their skills. "The workers define as unfair the situations and relationships that deprive them of their creativity . . . thus denouncing all of the impediments to self-realization in work."[2]

Robert Karasek, a professor at the University of Massachusetts School of Health and Environment and a leading American researcher in occupational health, has shown a close link between a person's autonomy and his/her mental and physical health. Karasek and his many associates worldwide have scientifically proven how toxic it is for personal well-being if people have no means to be creative and to develop their abilities, if they cannot decide how the work and duties are done and if they cannot participate in decision making.

When we carefully examine this problem, we see that occupational status or salary is no longer enough to motivate employees. The challenge now is to offer employees a chance to use their creative capacities and to give them a say in the work to be done and in company decisions that affect them directly or indirectly. Management should empower individuals to act. "But not just any action: the kind that people can recognize as coming from themselves, that fulfils their ideals and values and in which they feel responsible and independent."[3] Management should understand that work is not solely determined by the chain of command. It is constantly organized and reorganized by those who do it. Through awareness of this reality, autonomy and participation in decision making can more easily become management values and practices.

Autonomy and participation in decision making are also closely linked to recognition at work. When there is not enough autonomy or participation or none at all, many people experience a feeling of being invisible to the company's managers and senior executives. When an employee at a financial institution was left out of the decision-making process, this is how he felt:

> When decisions are imposed on us, it's as if we don't even exist. As far as management is concerned, we're not part of the decision-making process. We feel as if we've been ignored—a bit like not saying hello to the janitor who is cleaning up your office while you're still there!

In reflecting on this, we have come to the conclusion that it is through autonomy and participation in decision making that we publicly confirm our existence, experience and expertise in the eyes of others. We thereby raise an individual's value more concretely and credibly than through verbal recognition or a declaration (thanks, congratulations, honors, etc.). Through verbal recognition, we may shower someone with praise, but it is solely through autonomy and participation in decision making that the person's expertise is genuinely recognized. This is how individuals will see their power increased, for it is by participating in decision making that they may define the terms of their autonomy and involvement.

Indeed, an individual's value is recognized as much through autonomy and participation in decision making as through verbal recognition. It is also a sign of respect, as pointed out by this store manager: "When people ask me for my opinion on what is going right or going wrong with the customers, it's a great sign of recognition and respect!" By listening to employees, by establishing processes for consultation, by getting the affected parties involved in projects for organizational change, managers and senior executives can bring about a kind of active management that greatly promotes employee well-being and efficiency.

Despite the benefits to both the individual and the organization, autonomy and participation in decision making are perceived in many companies as a threat, a weakening of authority or a desire for self-management. And yet, to ask for more autonomy and participation is not the same thing as wanting complete freedom and rejecting authority. Fear not, your employees are not asking for power. When we listened to their requests, they used such words as "participating," "being listened to," "being able to express ourselves," "contributing," "working together" and "being made more responsible":

- "Senior management should be listening more to people who often have good ideas."
- "Consult an employee before making a decision that will have a long-term impact on his or her work."

- "Establish real participation in decision making. Too often, we're asked for our opinion, but it's then ignored."
- "Give decision-making power back to immediate supervisors."

Perhaps you may have noticed. By asking for autonomy and engagement, these employees are demonstrating initiative and motivation to help develop projects that concern them. Surprisingly, ambition is valued but autonomy is still feared in the world of managers. Yet both go hand in hand.

## AUTONOMY

Autonomy is defined as an individual's leeway in deciding how work should be done. It is also the capacity to be creative and to develop one's abilities. Today, the most striking examples of autonomy come from high-risk occupations, such as that of prison officers.[4]

A prison is an institution that isolates people deemed to be a danger to society. In the United States, there are over two million prisoners and nearly 500,000 guards. Canada has around 40,000 inmates and about 6000 correctional officers and France 63,000 inmates and around 23,000 prison guards. Such inmates are repeat offenders for minor crimes, perpetrators of voluntary or involuntary homicide, rapists or drug dealers. Each of them is assessed to determine how dangerous they are to themselves, to fellow inmates and to the staff. The classification is usually done in terms of the crime (theft, murder, drug dealing, rape, etc.) and the intent (voluntary, involuntary, conspiracy), as judged by the courts.

Although this classification helps determine where and how long the sentence will be served, it does not provide prison guards with enough information on the kind of person being incarcerated. If the inmates are doing time for a serious crime (murder or rape), they will not necessarily be the most dangerous and unruly ones in prison. In some cases, they may even be the ones who help things run smoothly in a prison environment. "A dangerous prison inmate is one with the following characteristics: he resists being overpowered, he threatens the physical or moral well-being of the guards . . . he exposes officers to possible sanctions . . . This is notably the case with crazies, psychos or madmen."[5]

Beyond official and legal criteria, prison guards give themselves leeway in determining how dangerous an inmate is, the type of behavior he will adopt and the kind of relationship they will establish with him. To find out whom he is dealing with, a guard will add other criteria: appearance, clothes, gait, body language, behavior toward other inmates and the leadership he exercises. Based on such clues, guards will determine the appropriate degree of surveillance, leeway and tolerance, the amount of information to be given and the punishments to be meted out. By using skills that go beyond the official criteria, they may adjust their work practices and give inmates more respect, act fairly, keep their commitments and navigate between coercion and freedom. It is largely the prison officer's autonomy that will maintain social peace in the prison and the security of inmates and staff.

By briefly describing the situation of prison guards, we hoped to identify four main aspects of autonomy. If autonomous, you can (1) display creativity and use your skills, (2) influence how your tasks are organized,

(3) make decisions independently and (4) co-define your working conditions.

## 1. Display creativity and use your skills

Creativity is not just a privilege of artists, craftsmen or business leaders. We have pointed out several times already that an employee works nearly 2000 hours per year. This experience provides a sound understanding of the situation and the problems encountered. Let us turn to another work environment: education. While discussing with some high-school teachers, we were clearly told the importance of using one's skills to offer the best possible education. Here is what they said:

Researcher: How do you deal with children who have more trouble learning?

Teacher A: We develop special techniques over the years. You need time to observe students, to know what they like to do, to identify the type of problem they have. Is it a problem with memory, dyslexia, attention or discipline?

Teacher B: These students matter and we want them to succeed. I think about this all the time. I read a lot about the subject to find teaching methods and new exercises. We discuss because some of us have already run into this kind of problem and we use their experience and skills.

Researcher: How do you feel when things work out?

Teacher A: First of all there is the child's response, which is very satisfying, and then the reaction of the parents, who see their child developing to its full potential.

Teacher B: You know, we are really creating something here. We start with a child who has serious learning problems and we help him develop like a normal child. We get enormous fulfilment from our work.

Researcher: How do you react to the plan to standardize how we deal with students who have trouble learning?

Teacher B: I'm not against it. As long as we can use our own experience as well and it doesn't come only from Department of Education specialists. I'd like to keep some room for maneuver because my experience has shown me that you have to use your imagination and that there isn't just one right method. After 15 years in this field I know how to do my job.

The above comments stress the importance of being able to create and use your own skills, for the sake of a more efficient organization and for your own well-being.

2. Influence how your tasks are organized

How autonomous is an employee? There are several clear and concrete signs: being able to set priorities and determine how tasks are organized or carried out and being able to decide which information is necessary. It is not routine practice to give employees such leeway, except in emergencies.

During work with electricity linemen, we noticed there were two systems of rules and exercise of authority. Normally, they had to follow all of the rules and guidelines. This is something they knew and generally agreed with. Nonetheless during major blackouts that affected thousands of residential and industrial customers, the exercise of authority was more flexible, with the work teams being told to reestablish power as fast as possible. Of course, the situation was not one of anarchy. The linemen were allowed to organize their activities, set their priorities and define the rules to be followed. Generally, everything went fine and the statistics even showed fewer work-related accidents during emergencies than during routine operations.

In seeking autonomy, you seek to expand permanently, and not occasionally, the zone of influence where you alone make work-related decisions free of supervision. The goal is freedom to organize your tasks or priorities within your zone of influence, without having to obtain permission from a manager. Managers are available, however, if a problem arises. Therein lies the difference between autonomy and delegation!

3. Make decisions independently

A case study example of workplace autonomy can be seen in a group of weaving machine operators in a textile factory. They worked the night shift and most were satisfied. During our discussions, they mentioned several advantages: no boss peering over their shoulders and telling them what to do, no engineers testing out new equipment or work methods, more autonomy and far fewer interruptions of production. Of course, there were disadvantages: being more isolated, not being as well informed about company life and having to put up with family or personal inconveniences. Nonetheless productivity was just as good at night as during the day.

This nighttime setup seemed to work the best, so it was investigated to see how production could be better organized during the day. With a group of night- and day-shift employees and two managers, we reviewed the tasks, the problems and the incidents. For each situation, we looked into decision-making processes and initiatives during the day and at night. We were astounded. On the day shift, an incident would involve more employees than it would on the night shift and would especially lead to longer production shutdowns (12 minutes during the day versus seven at night) because more people were consulted and had to give their opinion. We then drew up a list of production incidents and determined whether the employee could decide alone or had to call in the foreman. Once the list had become factory policy, the employees appreciated their broader and officially recognized latitude for decision making. Their immediate supervisors, despite initial fears of "cutting the workers too much slack," found the changes to be largely beneficial. They were bothered less often and the shutdowns were shorter. Some hesitations remained over the employees' ability to handle responsibility, but these fears eventually faded away.

The factory manager was pleasantly surprised and went so far as to ask that the same exercise be repeated in other departments. He had this comment: "Initially, I was rather worried about giving the workers so much leeway. Now I see they are up to the job and my managers are less bogged down in minor production decisions that don't really amount to time spent productively."

4. Co-define your working conditions
Autonomy is not just a matter of organizing your work more or assuming more responsibility. It is also a matter of empowering employees to manage their time at work and to define the conditions of doing work.

Quebec, for instance, has a healthcare system whose working conditions and especially work schedules raise serious issues of employee autonomy. For some years now, because of the shortage of nurses, overtime has been built into their schedules. Nurses are told they have no right to turn down overtime because of their code of ethics. Overtime by nurses has been rising 17 percent per year on average for the past eight years. Last year, Quebec nurses put in a total of three million hours of overtime. As a result, they are not just asking for better organization of work but also better hours of work, since their schedules are greatly affecting their physical and psychological health, their personal lives and their families. This demand must be addressed. At the very least, they should be given some leeway to accept or reject overtime.

Employees want more say in designing their working conditions. This may involve part-time work, flexible scheduling, shared work, working at home, accumulation of work time and scheduling of vacation periods. When such accommodations are possible, they feel the company is taking their needs and constraints into account. By being accommodating, the company also shows that it trusts its employees and is committed to their autonomy.

## PARTICIPATION IN DECISIONS

Participation in decisions means being able to influence your level of responsibility, to take part in decision making and to comment on information from your immediate supervisor and company management. In surveys of 17,000 employees, we have found that only 55 percent of all respondents felt they had influence over what happens in their organization and 62 percent felt their top management were not listening to their suggestions. By participating in decisions, employees can define their places within the organization, including their level of autonomy and how it will be applied. Through our experiences in the business world, we have found that few concrete strategies exist to bring employees into decision making. Aside from certain consultations from time to time on various subjects and the existence of some participatory mechanisms (e.g., occupational health and safety committees, technology change committees, etc.), there are seldom official processes for participation in decisions. It is up to each manager to bring or not to bring employees into these processes. We have also noticed that most companies handle this issue in a reactive mode, that is, employees who wish to voice an opinion can do so only by complaining to their manager, to the human resources department or to the body that represents them in their relations with the employer.

We recently hosted a problem-resolution group. Its members were sales reps from a medical equipment firm who said they were overworked. They had large territories to cover and their sales targets were continually being increased. Almost all of them were self-employed. They each decided the schedule they would follow, the clients they would meet and the activities they would organize in their regions. Their workplace was their home and their car. They had few opportunities to meet and talk about their work, successes or problems.

During a regional meeting, the discussions were tense and many sales reps were complaining about the heavy workload and lack of resources. After this meeting, which was difficult for everyone, we were called in to try and settle things. When we met with the employees, one of them summed up the situation:

The same thing happens at every regional meeting. We're given an overview of the past quarter, and then briefed on new products, marketing strategies and so on. The Director presented management's expectations and the targets for each of the products we handle. The problem is that these meetings always take place the same way. We walk away with new orders and tougher requirements. What's missing is that no one listens to us or pays attention to our experience in the field and our needs. Generally, there are few comments. People listen and don't respond. They know there's no point anyhow and it's also risky for their reputation. The real discussions take place after the regional meeting. We talk among ourselves on the way home or over the phone over the next few days.

They just wished to be heard. They were hoping their opinions and suggestions could influence the decisions being made about their work. On his way out of the meeting, one rep, who had hardly spoken a word, slipped us a piece of paper and said: "I don't like to get involved in this kind of meeting, but here are a few ideas that might be interesting." While putting our things away in the office, we took a few moments to read the sheet he had given us. It contained a dozen suggestions!

We were expecting this reaction, having spoken with the director before the group meeting. He was aware of the problems: "I have no choice but to pass on what management expects. I don't have any more power than they do and I too am overloaded. More work for them means more work for me as well. We're all in the same boat!" After hearing his side of the story, we suggested that the problem was probably at two levels: production targets seemed to be set for the reps without their being consulted and the regional meetings seemed to leave little room for discussion or exchange of views. We suggested dealing with the structure of the regional meetings and participation in decisions, since the workload problem could not be settled without first having effective mechanisms for participatory decision making. Intrigued, he asked us how participation by the sales reps could be improved. This can be done through: (1) the processes for employee consultation and (2) the manager's openness to employee suggestions.

1. Processes for employee consultation

All employees can contribute to company decision making if the consultation processes are clear and adequate. Our work often leads us to speak with trade workers, professionals, managers, technicians and researchers. All of them have special expertise, talents and know-how in their fields. Whenever we meet with individuals, teams or organizations that are experiencing problems, we suggest a process of discussing and listening where everyone can express his or her view of the problem and the solutions. The role is to bring all of these views together and to suggest alternatives based on my professional experience. A good consulting process should follow this sort of approach.

Here is a case in point. As part of an occupational health and safety assignment, we went with a foreman to a sawmill. At each workstation where we stopped, we spoke with the workers after telling them why we were there. They told us about the problems they had while suggesting almost as many solutions. We had a chance to talk with the mill's oldest employee, who had 35 years of seniority.

He explained how pieces of wood would get stuck on the machine and the safety problems that resulted. He also had a solution that seemed realistic. The foreman was astonished and he broke into our discussion to say he would send a technician to fix the problem. When we were about to leave the employee, we turned to him again and asked whether he had already spoken about the problem and the solution he had just put forward. His answer was clear: "Nobody is interested in our ideas here!" The foreman shrugged uneasily with a sheepish smile.

We brought up the example of this sawmill worker because we think most people have much more to offer than is generally thought. By providing a reassuring environment that encourages contribution, a business can benefit from everyone's expertise and experience. We have observed and realized over time that one can significantly improve most decisions by consulting all relevant members of an organization.

## 2. Manager's openness to employee suggestions

Consultation is both a process and a management philosophy. Some companies spend a lot of time establishing participatory processes and structures but very little educating and convincing managers and employees about their importance. Whenever we audit managerial practices in big businesses, we find that there may be committees, participatory procedures and times for consultation, but in one out of two companies these tools are unused and looked down upon by managers and employees alike. It is not enough to have mechanisms for participation. Participation must also be actively supported by the manager. A good manager who consults is not necessarily someone with good tools for consultation. It is someone who believes that employees can and should make a contribution.

This point is a real challenge: only 50 percent of all respondents in our surveys say their immediate supervisor encourages them to speak up whenever they disagree with a decision. Yet such openness to new ideas is critical, as explained this manager of a quality control department in an auto parts plant: "My role is not to lay down a solution. I listen to what the technicians have to say. I remember the facts they tell me and what I didn't know. I thus get a broad range of information and alternatives for a solution to the problem. Next, we look for a solution that seems to us to be the best one. We learn together. Of course, the final decision is up to me. I also have to make allowance for the company's overall situation and senior management's wishes. That's normal and the employees know it."

This manager's explanation shows that by aiming for participation in decisions we are not aiming for total employee autonomy. The goal is a good balance between leadership, which aims to get all members of the team involved, and supervision, which empowers the manager to use authority. This interdependence will be effective when both sides truly listen and show openness to each other—when they form a partnership. Such partnership will be possible when the people involved understand that decision making is not an individual process but rather one that includes other people.

Unfortunately, when the time comes to make a decision, many managers cut all communications with their employees until everything is finalized. Decision making,[6] however, is not slower and worse when the decision maker considers more information, more views, more options and more ideas. By bringing your employees on board, you are not going to act on each and every one of their ideas. You are going to listen to different viewpoints and, once the decision has been made, you will explain what has been retained from the ideas put forward. As a junior manager told us: "It's fine to ask for our opinions, but when we learn about the decision, we don't see our input or the reasons why our ideas were rejected. It seems to me that if you ask people for their views, the least you can do afterward is to explain the final decision to those people. But for us, it's always a one-way street!"

It is normal that participatory decision making initially seems foreign to managers, employees and the organization. You must learn to get to know each other, to give each other guidelines for discussions, to put aside your doubts and fears and to find the right times and right places. You must not shirk participation for lack of time or because the situation is urgent. After a while, people will have learned to know each other. They will better understand different viewpoints, discover new realities, grasp the magnitude of the problem and assess possible alternatives. Eventually, participation will become a habit, and gradually turn into a partnership that forms part of the daily routine.

## WHAT'S YOUR SITUATION?

There are some preconditions for autonomy and participation in decision making. Based on our experience, the most decisive practices are the following ones. By filling out this diagnostic tool, you may get a quick overview of your company's situation.

## DIAGNOSTIC CHART

| | |
|---|---|
| 100% | = We often take the lead in this practice—There is room for improvement, but very little. |
| 80% | = We take the lead in this practice—There is some room for improvement. |
| 70% | = We offer little leadership in this practice—We should improve. |
| 50% | = We are not leaders in this practice—There is clearly room for improvement. |
| 30% | = We are not at all leaders in this practice—There is a lot of room for improvement. |

| | Leader, manager and worker practices | Score (%) |
|---|---|---|
| Leader Practices | 1. Senior executives are in favor of everyone participating in and contributing to decision making among all concerned. | — |
| Leader Practices | 2. Senior executives promote a culture of cooperation among the staff. | — |
| Manager Practices | 3. There are processes for participation in decision making for organization-wide projects. | — |
| Manager Practices | 4. Managers are open-minded. They discuss and value employee suggestions. | — |
| Worker Practices | 5. Employees wish to take responsibility for their success, the success of their team and that of their organization. | — |
| Worker Practices | 6. Employees regularly use mechanisms made available to them for participation in decision making. | — |

Once you have completed your company diagnosis, use it as a vehicle to discuss some of the issues with colleagues (board of directors, management committee, work group, team meeting, etc.), to develop awareness of the importance of employee autonomy and participatory decision making. These discussions will generate ideas and feedback that will certainly assist you in planning and initiating changes.

## 10 Simple Actions

1. **Set up a process for participation in decision making**
   There should be a process for participation in decisions that involve employees. This participation should not be improvised. You need to develop a process and tools that may guide managers and workers through each step of the process.

2. **Encourage autonomous decision making**
   As a manager, you should encourage your employees to make decisions on their own. First, define the zone of autonomy, and regularly tell employees they may decide on their own. Reassure them and be supportive whenever they succeed or fail.

3. **Expand the zone of autonomy**
   Employee autonomy is not increased just by carrying out solutions or suggestions. It is increased by expanding what is called the "sphere of influence" or the "zone of autonomy and responsibilities." This sphere includes implementing an idea, changing a process and so forth. It is not an area where you may make decisions unilaterally. It is where you should work in concert with other levels

131

of decision making in the organization. Expanding this sphere should also be done while respecting the decision-making power of your immediate supervisor.

## 4. Reduce the number of controls

With new standards for ethics, quality, respect for the environment and good corporate governance, the past decade has seen a great increase in controls, checks and audits. This stepped-up surveillance may work against efficiency. Its effect has been to reduce autonomy and sap the decision-making power of individuals. So we should question the levels of control over work. Why should three different departments check an expense account? Why should four different authorities approve a training plan?

Keep track of levels of control and question their appropriateness with regard to employee autonomy and participatory decision making.

## 5. Trust your employees' skills

Employees know their work. They spend on average over 2000 hours a year working. Management should give employees more autonomy, and employees should assume more responsibility.

To this end, you will need not just principles and processes of participation in decision making. You will need, first and foremost, management values based on trust in your employees.

Such trust may be developed by

- sharing information with employees
- developing tasks that include employee autonomy
- clearly defining everyone's role, responsibilities and accountability
- recognizing employees when they succeed and supporting them when they fail.

## 6. Do not use urgency as an excuse

Urgency is a convenient excuse for a quick and one-sided decision. Too often, the problem is not lack of time but that participation in decision making was not done early enough in the process. Such participation should begin at a very early stage, and not when the decision, especially a final one, is about to be made.

## 7. Listen to the ideas of others

A concrete sign of participation is when one feels listened to during a discussion, debate or meeting. Too often, instead of listening, the others are preparing their answer, argument or objection. This attitude is not conducive to participation and is a clear sign of nonparticipation. So listen and follow up on comments from employees. Follow-up is a concrete sign that participation is working.

## 8. Promote a solution-oriented approach

Participation may mean speaking about problems encountered while working. You should especially zero in on what may be called a "solution-oriented approach." When a person raises a problem, he should also be encouraged to explore possible avenues to a solution. This is simple enough, just ask: "What do you think we should do to fix the problem?" Some managers even go so far as to ask for the solution before they have fully heard the problem!

## 9. Give decision-making power back to immediate supervisors

Often enough, employees will ask that more power be given to their immediate supervisor. They are not asking for more control. They want their manager and their team to have more autonomy and leeway. If authority is closer, there will be fewer delays in decision making and fewer problems left unsettled.

## 10. Do not change working conditions without consultation

People do not want the company to ask them about *every* decision, but they do wish to be consulted (*not* have a veto) over any decision that directly concerns them. When it is about a workspace, a procedure or a job schedule, you should consult the people concerned.

### KEY POINTS

- Autonomy is an individual's leeway to decide how work should be done, to decide what task should be carried out, to influence the level of responsibility and the possibility for creativity, and to develop abilities
- Participation in decisions is the ability to influence responsibilities, the possibility to participate in decision making and the opportunity to comment on information from one's immediate supervisor and senior management
- The possibility and ability to influence one's work is key to the well-being of people and the efficiency of organizations
- By allowing autonomy and participation in decisions, we also recognize the value of individuals and show respect
- The challenge for companies is to let employees each use their creativity, and have their say over the work to be done and the decisions to be made

- By influencing how work is done, we show how autonomous we are and how much we are respected for our skills
- Through autonomy, we give individuals leeway to factor in their own work-life balance and well-being, in addition to business efficiency
- When it comes to participation in decisions, most companies operate in a reactive mode, that is, if employees wish to complain, they may do so only by going to their manager or to a body that represents them in their relations with the employer (e.g. trade union)
- Most decisions could be significantly improved through consultation with members of the organization
- Some companies devote a lot of time to setting up processes and structures for participation and very little to educating and convincing managers and employees to use them
- Decision making is not slower or worse when the decision maker considers more information, more views, more options and more ideas

# CHAPTER 8

# CLARIFY EVERYONE'S ROLES

Just how important are these missing pieces of management? It may be useful here to draw an analogy between the world of sports and the world of business, particularly for the problem of task confusion and conflict that many employees and managers run into. A football team cannot allow two players to do the same play, to interfere with each other or, worse, to be unaware of whom exactly they should be covering. Otherwise, any strategy, however well planned, will run into trouble to the dismay of the spectators, the players and the coach.

In football, as in any sport, victory will depend not only on the skills of the players but also on the overall strategy, which is directed by the coach. This strategy, or "game plan," should be clearly communicated, should define each player's role and should be followed by everyone. It will largely determine whether the game is won or lost. A good strategy will not only lead the team to victory but also boost player morale.

The importance of strategy, and the care with which each player's tasks are defined, will apply just as much in the world of business. Unfortunately, many businesses experience role conflicts and ambiguities in defining employee tasks that would never be stood for on a pro sports team. We should understand that an organization's strategy is not just goals, action plans, production schedules and deliverables. A company and its managers should ensure that employee responsibilities, roles and tasks are clearly defined, and do not clash with each other. The work processes should be precise and clear. Everyone should know what he or she has to do, and everyone should strive for the same goals. When employees identify inconsistencies in their tasks, or say an assignment is no longer clear, the organization of work is hampered by role conflicts or role ambiguity.

Problems of role conflict or role ambiguity are not limited to employee tasks. They may also occur between departments, services and production units. For example, there are organizations where many people from different departments interact with a single client. Hospitals are a case in point. A rehabilitation center attendant highlighted how he coped with often divergent demands:

A patient's day is a very full one. He sees many hospital workers and I have to manage the multiple demands. The doctor wishes to see him late in the morning, but the physiotherapist just works mornings and has to do the rehabilitation exercises between 9 and 11:30 a.m. It's also the day for his bath. So I have to get him up very early to prepare him. I also have other patients to look after! I spend my day managing these conflicting situations. There should be better coordination among the different services. No one seems to take into consideration my needs or my patients' needs in order that I may do my job properly!

This example shows that it is not enough to provide an employee with a good job description. You also need to look at coordination of tasks among the employees and among divisions or departments.

To make things even more complex, an employee may experience role conflicts on the job that go well beyond the workplace. An employee or manager also has a life after work that may conflict with workplace requirements. For example, two teachers are married to each other and have a meeting in another town on the same day. Who will take care of the kids? Who will call the grandparents? Who will drop the out-of-town meeting? There are many such conflicts that can make employees less happy and businesses less productive.

These situations are legion and pose a serious problem. In our surveys, 47 percent of all respondents feel they are doing tasks that should be done differently. Moreover, 27 percent experience role ambiguity and say they have no clear idea how their boss wants them to manage their work time.

## HOW DO WE DEFINE ROLE CONFLICTS AND ROLE AMBIGUITY?

Take your time to understand this issue. In the following pages, we will answer several questions. How do we define role conflicts and role ambiguity? What forms do they mainly take in the workplace? What are their causes and consequences? What can we do to reduce such conflicts and ambiguities?

All work consists of a job description and a set of roles. Whether you are a doctor, a secretary, a truck driver or a financial analyst, we each have a role that has been assigned to us and that we perform through our actions and decisions. We may define a role as a set of expectations (behaviors, rules, goals, results) that are determined by a work dispatcher (the manager), by the work environment (coworkers, clients or suppliers) and by the receiver (the person who has to do the task). Since several people may define our role, dysfunction will regularly occur through role conflict or role ambiguity.

First, role conflict means a clash between at least two expectations. The classic example is a conflict between quantity of work and quality of work. Should a secretary work fast or properly? For a financial analyst, is it the number of products sold that counts or the quality of customer service? Should a doctor prevent or heal? For many people, such dilemmas come up every day. We can best identify role conflicts by looking at two components.

The first component is objective, that is, measurable. A secretary may explain that the number of requests for her services is keeping her from doing a job that meets quality standards. A financial analyst should see the direct relationship between higher sales targets and problems in providing after-sales service. A doctor should know that the latest budget cuts would just lengthen waiting lists and make it even harder to meet Department of Health objectives.

The second component is subjective and has more to do with the difference in perception between the work dispatcher and the employee. For example, a quality controller's role is not understood in the same way by the quality controller as it is by that person's boss. They each have differing expectations. The boss would like to see higher productivity, but the controller knows the quality of the work would suffer and job fatigue would increase.

To avoid this kind of situation, we should be aware that role conflict might take four forms:

1. Role conflicts due to one person making requests
2. Role conflicts due to several people making requests

3. Role conflicts limited to one person
4. Role conflicts between two departments.

1. Role conflicts due to one person making requests
Such conflicts are often due to the incompatible expectations of one manager. For example, a manager will ask you
to do a job without giving the technical, human or financial resources you need. Here the conflict comes from a
single work dispatcher who asks for one thing but fails to
provide the other. Over the short or medium term, there
will be a role conflict that makes the task impossible or
leads to serious personal consequences. This was the case
with a carpenter we met during a study on occupational
safety at construction sites. The foreman had asked for
repairs to a cornice on the roof, but the scaffolding was
not high enough and the carpenter had to install a lad-
der on the scaffolding to reach the cornice. He knew he
was in violation of the safety code, but felt compelled to
do what the foreman told him. He hoped to do the job
without falling and without being caught by the safety
inspector. The foreman, meanwhile, had given an order
while knowing that the equipment was inadequate. He
too had no choice: the house was overdue for delivery by
several weeks.

2. Role conflicts due to several people making requests
Such conflicts take the form of contradictory requests
or goals from two work dispatchers. This situation is
increasingly common in industrial projects that involve
partners from several countries. For example, one partner may want the least expensive bidder on a subcon-
tract, while the local partner prefers suppliers he knows
and with whom he has had business relationships for

141

several years. This kind of situation causes tensions not only in internal project management but also in business relationships. Such conflicts may also occur within a single organization. This was the case with a train controller whose boss asked him to check all of the riders' tickets. The head of the train crew, however, advised him against jeopardizing his personal safety by insisting whenever a rider refused to pay.

Such conflicts also occur in hospitals. Several years ago, the father of a friend was hospitalized for a health problem. The members of his family were taking turns watching over him and providing personal care. This friend several times asked that his father be bathed regularly. He told us he had put a lot of pressure on the nursing staff and the head nurse. Worried about his father's well-being, he was making requests that differed from those of the hospital management, with the result that the attendants and nurses had to cope with two different sets of requests. He wanted a bath every other day, whereas the hospital felt that two baths per week were enough. On top of his requests were those of other families who were also taking care of their hospitalized loved ones. The nursing staff tried as best they could to reconcile all of these requests.

In our hospital assignments we have often heard staff say that the quality of care matters but that the number of patients and their unwieldiness made it hard to reconcile all of the requests from families and hospital management. One evening, a nurse told us: "I do the most I can. If the families feel that their child, father or mother don't get the care they should they can complain about the lack of staff. That might help us. We've often made such requests and got nowhere!" There is a key link here involving lack of resources, workload and the emergence of role conflict or role ambiguity.

## 3. Role conflicts limited to one person

Such conflicts are due to incompatibilities between the role to be assumed at work and personal roles, responsibilities or values. For instance, we routinely see small businesses where the owner/manager is also the father of an employee who performs poorly or fails to adopt the right customer strategy. Often, the father is stuck with a dilemma. Should he try to protect his business at the risk of a damaged relationship with his son? Should he let things slide to hang on to his son—the one who will eventually inherit the business? Whatever you may think, the choice is not so simple and the situation not so rare.

Such role conflicts also frequently arise among people with a strong sense of professionalism, who see any compromise or relaxation of quality criteria as a serious conflict between what they are expected to do and their personal or professional values. A nurse, for example, will experience this conflict if the son of a patient asks her for something that runs counter to the doctor's instructions. An accountant will have the same dilemma if asked to ignore certain financial transactions.

## 4. Role conflicts between two departments

Such conflicts are due to incompatibilities or divergences between two roles or two departments of the same business, for example between the marketing service that sells the products and the production service that has trouble keeping up with orders because of a lack of workers on the production line. Such conflicts affect not only business processes and business efficiency but also the employees of both departments, who have to contend with dissatisfaction from both sides.

## WHEN NOTHING IS CLEAR

Role ambiguity may result from lack of clarity about (a) what is expected, (b) the procedures/methods and (c) the benefits/consequences in the role. Ambiguous expectations arise at the level of goals, deliverables or delivery times. For example, a young summer intern at an engineering firm may be too timid to ask the boss to clarify the latest orders. Procedures or methods may also be unclear. Which procedures apply to settle a complaint, to process a purchase order or to divide up tasks between two administrative sections?

Finally, ambiguity may arise at the level of a project's benefits or a strategy's expected consequences. For instance, a manager may be asked to fix a problem with a major client, to settle a production problem or to introduce a change quickly without really defining the expected outcome. This situation was summed up to us by a manager in a consulting firm: "I was given an assignment, but I don't exactly know what management is expecting from me!"

We will now pursue our investigation a bit further and try to understand why role conflicts or ambiguities happen in work processes.

A leading cause is lack of autonomy—employees cannot make the changes they feel are needed to bring the theoretical job into line with the actual one. Excessively rigid tasks or lack of leeway make it impossible to organize tasks in line with how they are actually done. In the time we have spent with employees and managers, we have often heard them say the work should be done differently, tasks should be assigned on another basis or a work sequence should be rearranged. Too often, the same people tell us they cannot do anything because they are not authorized and lack the necessary power.

"Lack of supervision" is another factor that greatly contributes to role conflict or role ambiguity, since the manager does not know the work process well enough or is seldom around to understand how dysfunctional the employees' tasks are. Some years ago, some employees at a food distribution company suggested that several things were going wrong at work: each employee's responsibilities were poorly defined, deadlines differed from one supervisor to the next and the order of tasks seemed to be inconsistent. They pointed out that these problems had been dragging on for two years and had not been fixed yet. Their supervisor was seldom around. He had been given an important assignment to overhaul the production process of perishable goods. When the supervisor was around, he would hold a meeting with so many items on the agenda that it was actually an information meeting and not an opportunity to fix problems. The argument was always the same: "We aren't going to change anything now because the work process will soon be modernized." He had been making this comment for 18 months and the employees were still working in the same dysfunctional manner. They no longer believed in his promises of change, which they openly ridiculed.

*Role ambiguity may also arise when someone is in an unfamiliar environment.* This is often the case with part-time workers, substitutes and temps, who know their job but are unfamiliar with the work environment because it changes so often for them. A temporary secretary, for example, will not know exactly what she is expected to do. A nurse from a private agency will not know the patients' special needs or the doctors' routines. In either case, they will try to do their best, all the while not knowing whether their work is up to par or how they will adjust if criticized or complained about.

*A person whose expectations change regularly* may also cause ambiguities in the work to be done. Freelancers have to cope with constantly changing and not-always-clear expectations, since they are often called in during emergencies that leave little time to explain everything. Freelance journalists must adapt quickly to different editors, newspaper styles, readerships or TV viewers.

*A person whose ability to reach goals may depend on another person's behavior* may also be confronted with role ambiguity. This situation is common among teachers and managers who are assessed not only on their own achievements but also on those of their students or employees. The goals are not always clear and depend not only on the person who teaches or manages but also on the person who learns or does the work. The ambiguity lies in knowing what is to be expected and assessed.

*Role ambiguity also arises when a person gets no feedback on his work or gets it only over the long term.* One situation comes to mind. While leaving a meeting at a law firm late one evening, we had a chance to speak with the night watchman who would open the door to the main entrance. He was a young man, 27, who had been doing this night job for six months. When asked whether he liked the job, he said it was all right. We then asked whether he thought he was doing his job well. A bit taken aback, he replied: "I don't really know. I've only seen my boss twice and haven't heard of him since. I'd like to see him more often because there are several things I'm not sure about! I figure it's OK, though, because no news is good news!" He laughed as he opened the door. We suggested he leave a note for his boss, who worked days, to ask him for a meeting.

Resolving role conflicts and role ambiguity is key to having happier workers and a healthier business. Many managers realize they can improve working conditions by changing expectations and ways of doing work.

## WHAT'S YOUR SITUATION?

Certain conditions are needed to reduce role conflict or role ambiguity. Based on our experience, the most decisive practices are the following ones. By filling out this diagnostic chart, you may get a quick overview of your company's situation.

## DIAGNOSTIC CHART

| | |
|---|---|
| 100% | = We often take the lead in this practice—There is room for improvement, but very little. |
| 80% | = We take the lead in this practice—There is some room for improvement. |
| 70% | = We offer little leadership in this practice—We should improve. |
| 50% | = We are not leaders in this practice—There is clearly room for improvement. |
| 30% | = We are not at all leaders in this practice—There is a lot of room for improvement. |

| | Leader, manager and worker practices | Score (%) |
|---|---|---|
| **Leader Practices** | 1. Senior executives clearly define the assignments, areas of operation and power of the different departments. | — |
| | 2. Senior executives promote a culture of cooperation rather than competition among the different departments. | — |
| **Manager Practices** | 3. Meetings are regularly held between the different departments to discuss work processes. | — |
| | 4. Managers regularly set aside time to clarify and discuss their employees' tasks. | — |
| **Worker Practices** | 5. Employees feel free to ask for explanations whenever things are unclear. | — |
| | 6. Employees mutually agree to define their tasks and roles so as to facilitate the fluidity of work processes. | — |

Once you have completed your company diagnosis, talk it over among relevant people of your choosing (board of directors, management committee, work group, team meeting, etc.). This discussion should give rise to observations that will surely help you in planning and initiating changes.

# 10 Simple Actions

### 1. Clarify the roles of your team members
Quite often, one worker will not know what another one does, even when they work side by side. Or, they may

not know what work is being done by various upstream or downstream departments, shops or units. Such ignorance often makes people blame others for whatever goes wrong or think that others are wrong and cannot understand the situation. But that is how everyone thinks! So set aside time for meetings where people from your team or another can explain their work. Such get-togethers will help everyone exchange views about work or business.

2. **Clearly explain what you expect**

   Role conflict or role ambiguity generally arises because people do not know exactly what they have to do. Most employees will ask to be informed about their responsibilities, assignments or area of action. The problem is that there often is a gray area or, even worse, no one exactly knows where someone's work begins and ends. Effort is needed to define what is expected from employees and to discuss these expectations. A job description is a good starting point, but it must be rounded out with information on what is expected. Seldom does a job description fully portray what a person actually does.

3. **Do not defend unworkable procedures at any price**

   An assignment may run up against administrative rules that are inefficient or simply unworkable. Do not defend the system at any price and pretend that everything is fine. Listen to complaints and requests for change. Your employees know their jobs and usually have straightforward solutions. Your organization and reputation as a manager will be better if you are open to discussing problems than if you try to defend the system to everyone and against everyone.

## 4. Know what you need to do

A lot may happen in a business and will happen pretty fast. Managers will not always have enough time, willingness or ability to ask if everything is OK. Play a proactive role to clarify tasks. Feel free to see a higher-up to find out exactly what is expected. What are the exact deadlines? What is the desired level of quality? Have things changed in your assignment? If the tasks are unclear or if there is a conflict between competing requests, report the problem and discuss it with the right people.

## 5. Develop a mentoring system for new employees

A job description does not define the complete reality of a job. New employees will have many questions about their tasks, the sequence of operations, the purpose of each stage of production and so on. The first few months on a job are critical and may make all the difference in the way one perceives business goals and each person's tasks and roles. These points may be clarified by the manager or trainers. There are also senior staff— mentors who can guide new employees in learning the ropes. Such peers may reduce role conflicts and role ambiguity, thus making for happier employees and a more efficient company.

## 6. Coordinate requests

You can also clarify an employee's job by coordinating day-to-day requests. Increasingly, people have to reckon with multiple demands from managers, coworkers or different clients. To avoid conflicts in priorities or deadlines, a company may now offer a one-stop service, a help line or a dispatcher for more consistent management of requests.

## 7. Earmark the resources needed for the job

An employee or manager may run into trouble not just because the assignment or request is unclear but also because not enough resources are available. An employee, for instance, may have to serve more customers without a corresponding increase in working hours. Or he/she may be assigned a new task without any training. To resolve such role conflicts or role ambiguity, you must earmark the resources needed for new demands.

## 8. Define the actual job

A job description does not describe the entire job to be done. A simple exercise is to list all of the tasks associated with an assignment or workstation. Role conflicts and role ambiguities often lie in what is undefined. The strategy here is to harmonize tasks that are defined with those that are undefined and yet part of the job.

## 9. Regularly talk about work achievements

If people get little feedback about their work, they may think there is some kind of role conflict or role ambiguity. By regularly speaking about expected results that have been achieved, you will also address the content of the work. Such a discussion will enable you to harmonize the manager's needs with the employee's needs.

## 10. Encourage discussions among different departments

To reduce role ambiguity and role conflict, ensure that information circulates laterally among different services, departments or units. To this end, organize interdepartmental meetings where people can explain what they do. What are their limitations? What vision do they have of work? What are their needs? The aim here is not to confront but to inform. Once mutual understanding has been achieved, this kind of meeting can identify the actions needed to facilitate the flow of work and to reduce role conflicts and role ambiguity.

## KEY POINTS

- A role is a set of expectations (types of conduct, rules, goals, results) determined by the person who assigns the work (manager), by the work environment (coworkers, customers or suppliers) and by the person who is assigned the work (employee), according to company guidelines
- Role conflict occurs when two or more expectations clash with each other
- Role ambiguity is lack of clarity in the expectations, the procedures/methods and the benefits/consequences that are associated with a role
- Lack of autonomy keeps a worker from bringing his/ her role into line with the actual job to be done
- Lack of supervision contributes to role conflict or role ambiguity, since the manager does not know the work process well enough to identify any dysfunctions in the tasks

# CHAPTER 9

# MOVE FROM WORDS TO ACTION

Beyond the facts, evidence, advice and examples we have presented so far, how can we ensure that positive changes are made to the working conditions of employees and managers? What are the final recommendations for going from words to action? Real-world action should not be improvised.

International research on change, whether organizational, societal or individual, has shown that it is not enough to be aware of a problem or danger for things to change and that it is not enough to have advice, alternatives or solutions. The campaign "against smoking" is a concrete example of the need to go beyond the stage of information and recommendations. Indeed, it has long been established that cigarette smoking greatly increases the risk of cancer, and we have long had numerous ways to stop smoking. Yet many people still smoke. This finding may be extended to many workplaces, where people know the problems and how to fix them, and yet nothing ever gets done. For example, we know that lack of recognition saps motivation, that overwork increases stress, that interpersonal conflict hinders cooperation, that all of these situations taken together will undermine a company's well-being and efficiency. Yet, in all too many workplaces, nothing is done. We have regularly noticed that it is not for want of knowing the solution that nothing gets done. It is for want of knowing how to go about initiating change.

This was the problem of the owner of a medium-sized boot-making company.[1] In response to customer needs and market pressures, he decided to bring in a modular organization of work that would replace a traditional assembly line where employees performed the same task daylong at the same machine. The new task organization would be more versatile and increase productivity. According to Nicole Vézina, a professor at the University of Quebec in Montreal: "By reorganizing its employees in this way, the company sought to create a series of modular mini-plants for all phases of production. Operators were assigned not to a particular station but to a sector corresponding to their position in the sequence of operations."

With this mode of production, the company wished to provide its employees with a greater variety of work, more responsibilities and fewer repetitive tasks.

The employees did not react as expected. Right from the start, several problems appeared: increased fatigue because they had to stand while working, too much reliance on coworkers, trouble communicating among employees and strained work climate. The boss failed to understand what was happening despite his good intentions. Nicole Vézina and her researchers showed that the problem lay not in the solution but in its implementation:

> Implementation of organizational change of this magnitude requires a mix of staff training, adjustments to mechanical equipment and changes to the company's structures and culture . . . There had thus been

underestimation of such factors as the time needed to adapt to a new system and to go from individual work to group work, the time to learn and become more versatile and the support time to help them balance their mix of tasks at the modules.

This example shows you have to go beyond the stage of describing problems and listing solutions. You should look more into how to implement changes that will lead to real improvements. Some factors may be levers or obstacles. It is up to you to turn them into keys to success.

## KEYS TO SUCCESS

### Lever #1   Use a risk management approach

You may find the 7 missing pieces of management in this book to be pretty obvious. This does not mean that foresight is unnecessary. In fact, planning is something that no company can afford to improvise or neglect. Too many organizations ignore risk management and opt for what we call "flying blind"—an approach where problems are not clearly identified and where the favorite idea is not always the most effective one. To act more seriously and effectively, there are three possible strategies:

### 1. Analyze the company's administrative data

To size up the seriousness of your problems, first find as much administrative data as possible (on absenteeism, types of absenteeism, employment insurance, payroll costs, etc.). Such data may vary from one company to the next, and will include information on short- and long-term disabilities, costs of employment insurance, consumption of prescription drugs, psychotherapy and reasons for using the employee assistance program. Data may be available for the company as a whole and for each department—this being key to targeting of problem areas. We have found that administrative data matter a lot because, as management indicators, they will help guide your initial decisions and later ones as well. Furthermore, by producing a readable chart from such data, you will be better able to dispel doubts about how serious the company's problems really are.

## 2. Use focus groups or individual interviews

If no administrative data are available, this being often the case in a small business, you may wish to use information from focus groups or individual interviews to target the main problems and the departments the most at risk.

For example, after being called in to resolve a conflict between a head nurse and her team, we asked the hospital's management to bring together its managers to identify the other "hot spots" in the institution. After an hour together, without using administrative data or any kind of survey, eight situations were identified as being likely sources of conflict. Managers know their staff and know where the "hot spots" are (i.e., repeated grievances, rumors, quarrels among employees, etc.).

If you use this more informal method, be careful. Many people are aware of a problem while not always knowing its actual extent or consequences. So the risk is not so much in being unaware as in misjudging the extent (i.e., number of employees affected) and the consequences (demotivation, absenteeism, presenteeism, etc.). Despite these obstacles, small and medium-sized organizations find that focus groups and individual interviews are an excellent means to identify problems that undermine a company's well-being and efficiency.

### 3. Survey the employees

In a large company or when administrative data are unavailable in a smaller one, a survey may be a useful option. Surveying will help you plan strategy by quantifying the problems and how they affect both the employees and the organization.

## Lever #2   Financial support of a business

Support from management matters a lot, especially when it is financial and substantial. Working conditions cannot be improved without some investment. This may involve freeing up work time, hiring a trainer, consulting an expert, overhauling work procedures and so on. Do not make the mistake of providing a budget only for the phase of diagnosing the problem and developing solutions. In many organizational change programs there is no budget available for implementing solutions and following them up. Yet this is the most important phase— the one where improvements actually take place.

Once a specific budget has been earmarked, the project will become much more credible, opportunities for action will open up and support for implementation may be envisaged. As part of an action research project we conducted, a company provided a £100,000 annual budget for activities to improve employee psychological health. The budget showed it took the problem seriously, was providing actual financial support and wished to motivate employees and managers alike to take an active part. During the next 18 months, the company could regularly point to this support to answer criticisms from different people within the organization. Money talks. It shows you mean business.

## Lever #3   Support managers when introducing changes

In some cases, changes may affect delicate aspects of an organization: tasks, human relations, decision-making processes and circulation of information. When managers push through with these changes locally, in conjunction with their employees, they may not always have the requisite skills or abilities. The employees, in turn, may be under much stress and have heavy workloads. Many organizations therefore need consultancy advice from outside to support their change activities, particularly from highly credible advisers. There are many examples of successful collaborations.

## Lever #4   Integrate changes into a broader organizational project

Improving working conditions is usually a project that is ad hoc, temporary or done in parallel within an organization. Such a project carries less weight in overall strategy than do regular production activities, financial commitments or competitors. As much as possible, you should integrate it into your organization's broader strategy (i.e., mission, strategic policy aims, development plan, etc.) to consolidate support from management. This integration will make the project a higher priority and help guarantee its implementation and long-term existence, as opposed to leaving it in the hands of a short-lived committee. This was the case with a major forest industry firm that decided to integrate employee well-being into its corporate goals. Management regularly had to report on this subgoal, and not just talk about it when things were going poorly. Employee well-being became central to the firm's strategy and its efforts to become more competitive.

## Lever #5    Use a participatory approach

By bringing employees and managers into the project to identify problems and implement solutions, you are increasing its chances of success. These people are experts on their work situation. Project success thus does not hinge solely on commitment from management. When dealing with a specific unit (i.e., department, division, shop, etc.), you will need support from the manager in order to mobilize the people under him/her and get their commitment. By first mobilizing management at the unit level, you will have support in implementing solutions.

In addition to support from the senior executives and unit-level managers, you will also need backing from the union. Union representatives can co-define the framework, rules and type of action in conjunction with employer representatives. They will thus actively help make the operating rules of the committees that will introduce the changes and the terms and conditions of the changes themselves. Their participation will clearly enrich this effort and thereby make the activities more credible to the employees. In short, employee participation is essential to success. Nonetheless, for such participation to be effective, you should boost your chances by ensuring that the participants have certain abilities.

- Desire to be active in the project
- Good practical knowledge of work environment
- Ability to consult with and mobilize employees
- Good judgment and open mind
- Creativity and communicativeness
- Desire to learn and to share knowledge
- Ability to work on a team
- Attendance at all meetings (availability)
- Proficiency in speaking in a group.

**Lever #6   Publicize the actions**

Marketing is critical during any change program. We are regularly told by people (employees and managers) that the organization was doing little for employee well-being. In many cases, much effort had been made but they were unaware. So do a good marketing job. Just because something has been done is no guarantee that people will know about it. Whatever is agreed should be communicated and communicated and communicated.

**AN OBSTACLE COURSE**

When planning strategy to improve employee well-being and business efficiency, make sure you know not only the levers for change but also the obstacles to change.

## Obstacle #1   Managers have excessively heavy workload

The workload chapter showed how overloaded managers are, and how much trouble they have doing all of what they plan to do. This problem has a perverse effect. It not only undermines individual well-being and business efficiency but also blocks efforts to turn things around because there is too little time or too much work. We face a paradox where managers (and often employees too) are overworked and preoccupied with day-to-day demands, and find it difficult to free up time and energy to improve working conditions. The result is a vicious circle that makes it impossible to think about problems and act on them. There is no other choice than to put up with the problems. Thus, overwork has a double impact: it impairs both personal well-being and efforts to introduce positive changes.

## Obstacle #2   Managers cannot manage change

Generally speaking, managers do not have all of the skills and abilities needed to manage change. They are people with an excellent knowledge of their industry, product or service, but they have limited knowledge of the ways to manage change. Paradoxically, they may thus become an obstacle. In almost every case, you will have to accompany the manager to ensure your efforts are carried out properly to achieve the expected results. This point must be part of project management. Be concerned not only about the changes to be made but also about the people who will make them. Usually, little thought is given to the support the manager will need to introduce change, to answer the employees' arguments, to handle difficult situations and so on. Besides increasing the chances of success, support is also important to the manager's psychological health.

### Obstacle #3   Employees and managers have negative opinions of proposed changes

Improving well-being on the job is a noble goal that may seem self-evident. Yet, from our observations in the field, we have found this is not always the view of employees and managers. Many of them openly doubted the success or purpose of such efforts. They often pointed to previous experiences with projects that had failed or not worked out as expected. This was not just resistance to change. It was doubt, based on experience. It is important, therefore, to rebuild employee and manager confidence. This rebuilding will require acting quickly and visibly to show the good intentions of the program to improve well-being in the workplace. A climate of good faith will also be created through the participation of both employees and managers. As well, to implement change, show patience and be ready to face negative opinions and comments about what is being done. Management too should show its support by acting quickly and decisively. With such projects, delay and foot-dragging will undermine credibility.

### Obstacle #4   Too much is attempted all at once

With many preventive actions taking place in the workplace (ergonomics, workplace psychology, conflict prevention, prevention of workplace accidents, etc.), identifying the risks is one of the first steps. This step is essential and will provide you with an inventory of all risks.

Generally speaking, the next step is to identify solutions. For each risk, one or more solutions are devised. This often involves writing up a report that sets out the problems and the corresponding potential solutions. We have found that in some participating organizations there were 60 or even 120 solutions per work unit. This number shows the range of possibilities for transforming work. It also shows that the problem-resolution groups have done their job.

Problems arise, however, when the time comes to carry out the solutions. There are often so many that the employees or managers become discouraged and the project itself may paradoxically lose credibility, since it is almost impossible to implement all of the solutions. We know that everyone has a significant workload. Consequently, an excess of solutions may cause actions to be diluted or simply ignored. When confronted with this problem, it is important to prioritize the possible solutions and reduce them down to three or four only. Certainly, not all solutions work out in any event, but experience has shown that when too many solutions are identified, very few actually get implemented. By limiting them to a small number, the chances of success will be greater, your effort will be less strenuous and any arguments over heavier workloads will be harder to make. The other solutions are not eliminated; they are simply put aside and may be used later. This step-by-step approach will increase your overall likelihood of success.

## Obstacle #5   Solutions have a limited shelf life

To improve company well-being and efficiency, it will always be necessary to invest time, money and human resources while creating expectations that need to be met.

Even if the changes are widely accepted, a major challenge will be to make sure they last.

Long-term viability is a big concern for management, unions and employees, who wish to see their limited resources invested effectively and efficiently. Moreover, if you initiate something and then end it abruptly, employees and managers alike will be less committed to future initiatives.

As a rule, people are especially concerned about the impact of any initiative and less so, if at all, about its medium- to long-term viability. No solution, of course, will last forever. The organization will change, as will the people. Better solutions will become available. The problem itself may change or disappear. Nonetheless, these are not the reasons why solutions fall by the wayside. The reasons typically are:

- Budgets have been cut or not continued
- The project leader has left and no replacement appointed
- The employees and managers have lost interest
- Other problems have become higher priorities.

How, then, can solutions be made viable over the long term? Here are a few ideas:

- Plan for the long term
- Ensure funding for the long and medium term, and not just for one year
- Plan for the departure and replacement of key people
- Integrate the initiatives into corporate strategies
- Appoint a senior executive to pilot the initiatives
- Keep the initiatives credible

- Give employees and managers the skills they need to take charge of the initiatives
- Assess the problem regularly
- Set company-wide or nationwide targets
- Ensure that the program for change is handled by a stable, mature department with a broad zone of influence
- Ensure the program has a high profile throughout the organization.

# 10 Simple Actions

### 1. Eliminate risks at the source

In occupational health and safety, the greatest advances have been in introducing preventive measures to eliminate risks at the source. The same kind of measure is needed for employee well-being. By going to the source, businesses can make lasting changes to working conditions. This is where risks are best controlled.

To guide your efforts, ask this question about any suggestion: Is this how the risk will be eliminated? If the answer is "no," keep on looking, instead of trying a solution that will lead nowhere and waste time, people and money.

### 2. Adopt the "2,000 working hours" principle

It is not always easy to choose the best preventive solution. The risk is to choose one that will have little impact on the workforce or the workplace. When judging a potential solution, the key criterion is how long it will last and how many people will be affected. This is what we call the "2,000 working hours" criterion.

165

In other words, the less you expose the workers to the risk, the better the solution will be.

For any solution, ask yourself: How many hours of work will be improved by the solution? For instance, a lunchtime conference will have an effect for a week or two, whereas a better distribution of tasks will have an impact over an entire year. The choice is clear.

**3. Ensure that resources are available for your goals**
Problem solving is an effective approach, but it has the flaw of focusing too much on looking for a solution and then stopping once a solution has been found. It is not simply because they are bad, inadequate or unrealistic that many solutions fail to be carried out.

Usually, the reason is a lack of human, financial or technical resources. During problem-solving meetings, you should push the questioning a bit further. Once the solutions have been identified, ask whether there are enough resources and also how long the resources will be needed.

**4. Ready, set, go!**
In any project to improve working conditions, it is essential and relatively easy to diagnose the problem, to analyze the data and to look for solutions. You then have to move quickly to the next stage: action and implementation. Generally speaking, too much time is spent on problem diagnosis and not enough on solution implementation. You need to show the employees that working conditions are improved not just by forming a committee but also through concrete action.

It is now time to act. Be wary of individuals who nitpick, who continually question the choices made time and again or who imagine all kinds of possible difficulties.

You should not act blindly, but it is impossible to foresee everything. If you wait too long before acting, the project will lose its credibility and the company will lose interest. Too often, committees fail to grasp that the ultimate goal is not to foresee everything but to carry out changes as soon as possible and to show the employees that the project is more than just words.

## 5. Use your leeway

It is untrue that we cannot change the way work is organized. The world of work is constantly changing. People say so all the time. It is the direction of change you need to influence. Both managers and employees have leeway they should feel free to use.

## 6. Adopt a participatory approach

It is not just up to management or to the union to improve well-being in the workplace. You need to get all of the personnel (employees and managers) on board as early as possible. This involvement should start when the problem is being diagnosed and not once the solutions have been decided on.

Having participants in and of itself is not, however, enough. Much will depend on their skills. You should (1) select them carefully and (2) train the ones who will help improve employee well-being.

## 7. Identify a champion

Improving employee well-being is seldom perceived and experienced as a company's first priority. This is normal and there is no point in fighting it. To give this priority a leading place, identify someone who agrees on its importance. This person should have good leadership qualities, a position of authority and an excellent network of influence.

Once you have picked this champion, make sure he or she stays in the loop, is kept informed and has the necessary exposure and recognition.

## 8. Do case studies

Employee well-being may be closely linked to business efficiency, but this hardly means that your company will automatically change the way it organizes work.

As with other projects (relating to technology, the environment or marketing), you should prepare a "business case" to show the extent of the problems, to justify changes and to identify the human, organizational and financial gains. Define employee and manager roles, and provide for alternatives to the plans you suggest.

## 9. Make employee well-being a criterion of managerial decision making

Personal well-being should not concern only the departments of occupational health or human resources. It should concern all departments. This human factor must be present in all decisions, all workstation designs, all work methods and all business processes. It should not be simply a value but also a decision-making criterion on the same level as business performance, customer satisfaction and managerial concerns.

## 10. Manage expectations

Although employee well-being is a worthy goal, it is important to avoid raising false hopes among employees and managers. Give an idea of what could be done and what will be harder to do or even impossible. It is better to present a realistic project than to stir up false hopes and risk undermining the credibility of your initiative.

# NOTES

## INTRODUCTION

1. To make this book easier to read, we have written it in the first person plural. We hope this choice will help the reader appreciate the experiences we have had with employees and managers in hundreds of organizations.

## 1 DISCOVER THE MISSING PIECES OF MANAGEMENT

1. Adkins, J. A., Quick, J. C. & Moe, K. O. (2000). Building world-class performance in changing times. In L. R. Murphy & C. L. Cooper (Eds), *Healthy and productive work: An international perspective* (pp. 107–32). London: Taylor & Francis.

2. Spector, P. E. (1997). *Job satisfaction: Application, assessment, cause, and consequences.* Thousand Oaks, CA: Sage.

3. Vandenberg, R. J., Richardson, H. A. & Eastman, L. J. (1999). The impact of high involvement work processes on organizational effectiveness: A second-order latent variable approach. *Group and Organization Management, 24,* 300–39.

4. Mathieu, J. & Zajac, D. (1990). A review and meta-analysis of the antecedents, correlates, and consequences of organisational commitment. *Psychological Bulletin, 108,* 171–94.

5. Cooper, C. L. (1994). The costs of healthy work organizations. In C. L. Cooper & S. Williams, (Eds), *Creating healthy work organizations* (pp. 1–5). Chichester, England: Wiley.

6. Heskett, J. L., Sasser, W. E. & Schlesinger, L. A. (1997). *The service profit chain: How leading companies link profit and growth to loyalty, satisfaction, and value.* New York: Free Press.

7. Schneider, B., Hanges, P. J., Smith, D. B. & Salvaggio, A. N. (2003). Which comes first: Employee attitudes or organizational

financial and market performance? *Journal of Applied Psychology*, 88, 836–51.

## 2 RECOGNIZE YOUR EMPLOYEES: A SIMPLE ACT

1. Collins, J. (2001). *Good to great*. London: Random House.

2. Mercer, Human Resource Consulting. (2005). Mercer snapshot survey: Measuring the return on total rewards: 2005 update, August .

3. Brun, J-P. (2008). An analysis of employee recognition: Perspectives on human resources practices. *International Journal of Human Resources Management*, April, 19(3), 716–30.

4. Siegrist, J. (1996). Adverse health effects of high-effort/low-reward conditions. *Journal of Occupational Health Psychology*, 1, 27–41.

5. Brun, J-P., Biron, C., Martel, J. & Ivers, H. (2003). Évaluation de la Santé Mentale au Travail : Une Analyse des Pratiques de Gestion des Ressources Humaines (Assessment of Occupational Mental Health: An Analysis of Human Resources Management Practices) (Études et recherches / Rapport No. R-342). Québec, Canada: Institut de recherche Robert-Sauvé en santé et en sécurité du travail.

6. Stansfeld, S., Head, J. & Marmot, M. (2000). Work-related factors and ill health: The Whitehall II study. Contract research report 266/2000. Health & Safety Executive. Sudbury: HSE Books.

## 3 SUPPORT YOUR EMPLOYEES

1. Berkman, L. (1985). The relationship of social networks and social support to morbidity and mortality. In S. Cohen & S. Syme (Eds), *Social Support and Health*, New York: Academic Press, pp. 241–62.

## 4 DEVELOP A CULTURE OF RESPECT

1. Forni, P. M. (2002). *Choosing civility: The 25 rules of considerate conduct*. New York: St. Martin's Press.

2. Pearson, C. M., Andersson, L. M. & Porath, C. L. (2000). Assessing and attacking workplace incivility. *Organizational Dynamics*, 29(2), 123–37.

3. Brun, J. P. & Kedl, E. (2006). Porter plainte pour harcèlement psychologique au travail : un récit difficile. *Relations industrielles / Industrial Relations*, 61(3), 381–407.

## 5   RECONCILE WORK WITH PERSONAL LIFE

1. SOM survey conducted in 2007 for Desjardins Société Financière.

2. Duxbury, L. & Higgins, C. (2001). *Work-life balance in the new millennium: Where are we? Where do we need to go?* RCRPP, n. W/12. Ottawa, Website: http://www.cprn.org.

3. Frone, M. R. (2003). Work-family balance. In J. C. Quick & L. E. Tetrick (Eds), *Handbook of Occupational Health Psychology* (pp. 143–62). Washington, DC: APA.

## 6   CONTROL THE WORKLOAD

1. Ricci, J. A., Chee, E., Lorandeau, A. L. & Berger, J. (2007). Fatigue in the U. S. workforce: Prevalence and implications for lost productive work time. *Journal of Occupational and Environmental Medicine*, 49(1), 1–10.

2. The model presented below is based on: Falzon, P. & Sauvagnac, C. (2004). Charge de travail et stress. In *Fondements théoriques et cadres conceptuels* (pp. 175–90). Paris, France: PUF.

## 7   ENCOURAGE AND SUPPORT AUTONOMY AND PARTICI-PATION IN DECISION MAKING

1. Dubet, F. (2006). *Injustices*. Paris: Seuil.

2. Dubet, F. op. cit., p. 26.

3. Lhuilier, D. (2006). *Cliniques du travail*, Paris, Érès, p. 86.

4. Lhulier, D. (1997). *L'univers pénitentiaire: du côté des surveillants de prison*, Paris, Desclée de Brouwer.

5. Lhulier, D. (2006). *Cliniques du travail*, Paris, Érès, pp. 116–17.

6. Eisenhardt, K. M. (1989). Making fast strategic decisions in high-velocity environments. *The Academy of Management Journal*, 32(3), 543–76.

## 9  MOVE FROM WORDS TO ACTION

1. Vézina, N., Stock, S. R., Saint-Jacques, Y., Boucher, M., Lemaire, J. & Trudel, C. (1998). Problèmes musculo-squelettiques et organisation modulaire du travail dans une usine de fabrication de bottes. Collection Études et Recherches – IRSST, Résumé, R-199, 28 pages.

# INDEX